"If you don't give up,
You haven't lost."

-Amish Proverb

I believe strength can only be found when there is peace inside your heart.

I believe there's no more important job and no higher priority than raising a child.

I believe animals are earths angels, here to teach responsibility, patience, unconditional love and loss.

I believe our response to others actions shows our true character.

I believe in closing one door before opening another.

I believe the simplest things in life make us the happiest.

I believe charity work should be done for God, not for recognition.

I believe love never dies, hope never ends and that inspiration is everywhere.

~Lori Wood

Dedicated To:

My Twin Brother
Larry Emerson

For making everything feel okay
when it all feels so wrong.

Amish
Above The Law 2

Karma Farm

A knock at the door
told us
it wasn't over.

Table of Contents

1
Windows

As I looked out the bedroom window of our new home into the clear summer night it felt like I was standing in my room at my parents' home. Felt like I was 12 again, peering into that night sky and vowing to myself I'd always remember what I saw so many times through that window.

I'd remember the sound of the frogs in the pond and the smell of the air. I'd remember the peace it brought me. I'd wonder to myself, when I grew older, would looking out a window into the night be as special as it was in those moments of my childhood? A mental time capsule I held on to.

The capsule had opened. There it was after all of those years. The big dipper. In the same sky, in the same place and for the first time since I was a kid, it was visible to me each night before I climbed into bed, just as it was from the upstairs bedroom window of the house I grew up in. This is where a long hard life full of twists and turns had taken me. This is where I was meant to be. That big dipper told me so, every night.

Many nights I'd lay awake in bed listening to the sounds of summer before drifting off. An occasional familiar sound would break into the night air. Clip clop, clip clop. The sound would peak and then fade away as an Amish buggy made its way up or down the hill and past our farm. Being a night owl with a bedtime in the wee hours, the sound intrigued me. I had always thought of the Amish as going to bed early after a long hard day's work and then back up at the crack of dawn to do it again. I decided I needed to draw a personal line between educating myself on Amish life and being just plain nosey. I enjoyed the sounds of the hooves as they echoed off into the night. I would leave it at that.

That personal line came easy to mind at times, hard at other times. Shortly after we moved into the house, we were moving an old broken and battered roll top desk. Unsalvageable, it had been left behind in the living room.

We took it to the porch to dismantle it. There were still crayons and tiny children's trinkets in the working drawers along with an assortment of pins, screws and worn out pencils. I pulled out drawer by drawer and stacked them in a pile so that Dan could carry them off to the burn pit.

As I knelt down to remove the final drawer something caught my eye. I reached in and pulled out a fist full of papers. Long forgotten and wadded up into the back of a now absent drawer. Receipts. Letters. Empty envelopes. Stacking them all up, I headed to the kitchen and grabbed a used plastic bag from the grocery store. I stuffed the papers inside it, tying it shut and tossed the bag into my art room closet.

And then one night, I started to go through them. I sorted them out. I threw away the empty envelopes and receipts and started to read the letters. They were personal. Some heart breaking. Some every day chatter. All very Amish, each one with a religious greeting at the beginning. Half way through the stack I put them all back in the bag and threw them into the trash can that sat beside the work area in my art room. As interesting as they were, they weren't my letters to read.

The view from my art rooms' window is both inspiring and intriguing. From the window on my right side, I looked out into the pasture and saw the animals. The horses and our goat, Pepper. Grazing, playing. Napping in the warm sun. On occasion I'd see our cats wandering through the grass in lure of a mouse or mole as if they were jungle lions stalking their prey. I could see the woods and beautiful unique trees and landscape that always made me sigh with contentment. I could hear the peepers from the pond at night and the thick harsh swallowing sounds of the larger frogs. There was peace outside that window. There was paradise out that window.

To the left of me the window exposed a view of the road and the Bishops property. Many things were seen from that window as well. Busy things. Dan's return home after a long day of work. A game of softball played by Amish children on a Sunday afternoon. Now and then a pasture full of beautiful Belgian horses enjoying time away from their harnesses. The Bishops children working hard pitch forking hay into a baler or chopping corn by hand to load it onto a wagon in the hot summer sun.

Endless Amish buggies rolling by as they went about their busy lives. An occasional barefoot parade of children and young women with head covering hiding the color of their hair but not the brightness of their smiles.

Amongst the traffic at times, the Bishop in his cart with a small Jack Russell always trailing behind him.

The theme that was played in the Wizard of Oz as the witch floated by Dorothy's spinning house on her broom stick, was like an unstoppable musical instrumental that always rang through my head as he passed by.

In my quiet corner I noticed that almost everyone who passed by looked at the farm. We had come a long way in such a short time. To us, the looks where compliments. We were proud our property was a head turner! We had both worked so hard. So many hours. The results were showing. We had taken our farm from being an eyesore to restoration. Although content with how far we had come in such a short amount of time there was still so much more to do. We prepared ourselves for a summer of hard work.

One particular day as I looked out the window to the left of me I was puzzled. Fog. Thick fog. Yes, it had rained but how come when I looked out into the pasture there was no fog? I stood up from my work and investigated the situation. The fog was rolling through the Bishops pasture and was so thick I could barely see his home. There was no fog in our pasture or the hills beyond it. I slipped on my barn boots and went outside.

The "fog" came from behind our shop and crossed the road. It went the whole length of the Bishops pasture, through his yard and directly to his home. It wasn't fog. It was smoke!

I walked across the lawn, down the length of the dirt driveway to the back of the shop where Dan was burning pine tree limbs, choosing to do so because it was safer to do in the wet weather.

"Dan, do you know where that smoke is going?" Before he even turned around to face me I could hear him burst out into laughter. He had a broad smile that told me he knew exactly where it was going. "Hey, I can't control where the smoke goes." Smiling myself, I agreed with him but suggested he takes the fire down a notch because the Bishops windows were open and it wasn't very nice to keep the fire up with the direction the smoke was going. Still smiling, he agreed. "Okay I'll tone the fire down a bit."

As I walked back to the house I was still smiling too. Not because of the smoke and the direction it was going. Because we continued to remain the kind of people we always were.

2
Strawberry Treasures

Writing Amish Above the Law felt like closure to a year full of so many emotional ups and downs. A new start. A possible means to rebuild us financially, one book sale at a time. Every small bit was going to help as we made our way through what felt like a field full of thorn trees and barbed wire. Someday we'd look back and see it all behind us with nothing but a field of forget-me-not. Some things are meant not to be dwelled on but to remind ourselves on occasion of how strong we really are.

When the book was published, the response was overwhelming to me. In my heart and mind I didn't know how to feel inside. Me? An author? They want me to sign their books? It all felt so crazy, like I was one person split into two. Had I really written that book they are talking about? The idea felt so foreign. An inner struggle that always left some sort of odd lump in my throat kept telling me "You're an artist, not a writer." I found myself saying that same thing out loud to a local reporter who had authored books of his own. His answer to me with a sweet smile was "Yes, you ARE a writer."

The reporter was brought into our lives through face book. It's such a small world. He ended up to be Dan's childhood softball coach. A kind man with a compassionate heart, I took pleasure in meeting him and talking with him. As he turned his recorder on for our interview he asked

"Is there anything you want said beyond all other things? Something you really want to stand out in this story?"

Without batting an eyelash I firmly said "Yes. There is. We want to make sure people know that we don't think that all Amish are alike. We have dealt with and have been friends with many Amish folks, for years. We don't group them together because of one or two bad apples and we hope that others don't either."

Our story was in the paper with a picture of Dan and me smiling and waving on the front porch. "Local Artist Writes Book: Release this

Friday." It wasn't long after that, there was a noticeable amount of traffic on the road to our farm.

We wondered what our Amish neighbors would think about the article in the paper. And what would they think about the book? How would they react to their Bishop being in the spotlight? Would they continue to smile and wave or would they digress to quietly going about their own business and pay no mind to us? Would they understand that we had nothing against them? Time would tell.

Dan tore out the overgrown herb garden that was close to the house and leveled it to become lawn. We both picked up a trailer full of rotted wood and junk that laid next to the corn crib behind the "store".

Inside the corn crib were loads of empty cardboard boxes and old corn cobs. That would be cleaned up another day. There was still so much to do.

Some days we'd be smiling and joking as we cleaned. Other days we'd shake our heads and feel angered that we were cleaning up a mess that we hadn't made. What kind of people were they to leave such a mess behind knowing someone else would have to clean it up?

Any treasure we found in the trash, we held on to. Counted our blessings for. The treasures weren't much. Maybe an old pot or jar. A useable bucket. A few sheets of siding thrown in the weeds and forgotten about.

My treasure was the strawberry patch behind the garage. I had been anxiously awaiting the berries I'd be picking.

During the contract period the previous summer, several Amish woman and children came to pick the berries.

I remembered the smiles as they told of collecting 100 quarts. "Do you want some of the berries?" They asked. I replied "No, with buying the farm and all, this year will be too hard to try and do anything with them. Next year though, when we're in and settled, I'm hoping to make some strawberry jam, if I can figure out how."

Several giggles emerged. "It's easy to do." The Amish women went on to explain how simple it was and assured me I could come to them for help if I needed it.

The strawberry patch was ours now and I had been watching it since early spring. It reminded me of my Dad and I thought about how happy he must be for me as he looked down from heaven and saw his little girl walking through those strawberry plants, trying not to step on any. Walking on her tippy toes and the sides of her boots at times as she clumsily made her way through that patch inspecting nature's treasures.

My Father made excellent strawberry jam and I was going to try my best to follow in those footsteps. I wished I could have had just one more day with him. I wished he were there to guide me. I knew one way or another, he would.

I attempted early on to weed but that idea quickly turned to defeat. It was too overgrown from being unattended for years and weeding wasn't in the realm of possibility. There were no rows. They were scattered everywhere.

When it was time to start picking them, the thorns and milkweeds were waist high. I would just have to do the best I could.

My picking companion was our black lab, Roxy. She loved the strawberry patch. As I carefully bent the thistles and milkweed over with my work boot to expose the berries close to the ground, I could hear Roxy sniffing with an occasional chomping noise.

Sometimes she'd get ahead of me and leave ripe red berries flattened and juiced into the dirt. That was okay. Couldn't help but smile at how that berry patch made us both so happy.

It had been hot and dry and the flowers I had planted in the beds by the house needed attention. I couldn't wait for the rain anymore.

Dan bought four hoses he could hook together and run from the barn to use for the fires he had behind the garage. He helped me to run the hoses to the house. Much needed water flowed over the flowers like a soft rain, helping them along until nature took over.

Life felt so good now. Reliving the previous summer while writing the book had taken an emotional toll on me. Now the book was written and out there. Time was moving on in an unknown but at the same time, in an exciting and refreshing new way.

I was in my own day dreamy world as I was using the hose in front of the house. I heard a strange noise on the dirt road. I knew it wasn't a horse or buggy. It sounded like a dragging type of noise. A Scuffing noise. Not an animal. What was it?

I turned toward the sound and saw an Amish man with his hands in his pockets and his head slightly tilted down. Our eyes met.

It was the Bishops Son. An awkward silence seemed to fill the air between us as we almost shyly scanned each other's face for a reaction. What was he there for? Was he going to confront me about the book? I didn't think so but I wasn't sure. He had never given us any problems and we liked him. He always seemed down to earth and genuine.

Reading his face assured me he wasn't there for trouble. "Hi, how are ya?" I said in an attempt to break the ice. "I'm good, thanks." After an awkward silence for what was probably only seconds but felt like minutes, he said "I was wondering if I could pick the strawberries, or maybe you have plans for them?"

I looked at our visitor and smiled. "It's so overgrown out there I don't think the patch is going to produce much. I plan to make strawberry jam with the berries I can find." In the back of my mind my thoughts were confused.

After everything that had happened in the past year did he really just ask if he could pick our strawberries? Did he want them for his families use or was he going to sell them?

Almost as quickly as those thoughts came, they were replaced by a reasoning voice within me. It was plain and simple. He wouldn't know unless he asked.

Dan came from around the house looking like a guard dog who was not yet sure who was talking with me. The Bishops Son looked much like a younger version of his father and dressed in Amish attire, it was hard to tell them apart at times.

When he saw it was the Bishops Son, Dan's steps slowed and a relaxed smile came over his face.

"Hi!" He said as he approached us. They shook hands. Although a heavy fog of awkwardness seemed to fill the air just as it had done only minutes before, it soon evaporated into idle chit chat between them with a smile here and there.

I chimed in. "Dan, maybe he will have some ideas on how we can move that store to the road."

Dan and the Bishops son began to discuss the move and how it could be done. New things were certainly being learned about moving an Amish built building. This was guy stuff.

I picked the hose back up and continued to water the flowers, making my way around the house and away from the men. I was wrapping up the hose when I heard their goodbyes and saw Dan coming toward me smiling. All was well.

"The Store"

3
450 Miles

A book signing along with an open house was suggested by a face book friend. What a great idea! Dan and I were excited to show off our house. The hidden bedroom hall way. The secret room. The Amish shower.

First things first. I had some major cleaning to do in our big fourteen room home.

I spent three days going from room to room in anticipation of company arriving. I knew all would not be perfect but I'd make it presentable.

We decided on the last Saturday in June from 2 until 6 PM. Those who wished to come would be free to take a tour or just sit and chat with us. We were both excited to meet new friends.

Dan would go into work that day until noon and then join me in the finishing touches of cleaning when he got home and as we awaited our first visitors.

I was rushing around the house that morning with a roll of paper towels and pledge, anxious and trying to assure myself the house would be fine. Did I get all the cob webs? What about the top of the dresser upstairs?

Dog hair on the Pergo floor caught my eye. I put the wood cleaner down and grabbed the broom. I still had to sweep. I still had to mop. There was so much left to do before our guests arrived.

I was on a mission to clean and in deep preoccupation when Roxy let out a bark and ran around the corner of the couch toward me. Hair standing up on her neck, making a barking sound while taking deep throaty breaths.

From poodle to Rottweiler in two seconds. That's Roxy. That's how she told me someone was at the door.

"Oh no, not yet. I'm not ready yet." I said to myself as I walked to the front door, with Roxy on my heels still huffing and excited with uncertainty. I peered through the doors window.

My first vision was that of a straw hat. It was an Amish man. Bending down I held on to Roxy's collar with one hand and opened the door with the other.

The person on the other side of our door was a handsome young Amish gentleman. Piercing blue eyes and black hair. Sharply dressed in clean pressed cloths. My mind raced as I tried to think of who he was. Had I seen him before? Did I know him? What did he want? Art work? Had he heard of the book and had questions? I smiled brightly trying to hide the question mark that was surely on my face as I said hello. I let Roxy's collar go and she sat loyally at my feet.

He introduced himself as the person who sold the farm to us. I felt a lump in my throat and a rush of anger I quickly forced back down into my soul. "Some Amish ministers from Ohio thought I should come here and sort this out with Dan and you to make things right. They came with me."

He nodded to the van parked beyond us, not too far away on the road.

Driven by an English driver, I could see Amish passengers.

The young Amish man's attitude and body language told me he was somewhere he did not want to be, doing something he did not want to do. It was clear to me that he may as well have said he was being forced against his will to come to us to make things right.

For a brief moment our exciting day of meeting people ran off its tracks and crashed. After that vicious settlement response letter that felt to us, like we were being laughed at, he comes knocking at our door not even trying to pretend he is sorry?

The key word was "brief moment." He and the Bishop had taken too much from us. I wouldn't allow any more.

I'd keep my peace within myself.

I started to speak. "You know, we wish none of this would have ever happened. All it would have taken was a little honesty." A flood gate opened as he began to ramble.

"I took the fence down in front of the house before you even looked at it because I didn't want buyers to see it and think the place looked junky" My heart skipped a beat.

Had he just lied again, in response to how things would have gone well, with a little honesty?

The fence wasn't ripped out of the ground until two months into our contract. I wanted so bad to go get the pictures and emails that would stop his dishonesty in its tracks. Instead, I continued to listen. I continued to keep peace within.

With a cocky smile he said "there wasn't a contract anyway." We knew that this was his motive during the sale. To seal the threat of a law suit against all of his wrong doings by not signing an extension to the contract. I swallowed against the large lump that was in my throat while I forced myself not to blurt out that the contract was reinstated by the black mail letter and the papers we both signed at closing.

I heard the van door shut and a young Amish woman climbed out and approached us. She was a beautiful girl with a peaches and cream complexion. A natural beauty with a preserved innocence about her.

I smiled at her and introduced myself. "You must be the Bishops Daughter." She smiled back and conferred as I went on to speak. "We got to know your Sister last year and we really liked her. We miss seeing her." My gaze had focused on the Bishops house.

Suddenly I felt an awkwardness overwhelm me and I was at a loss for words for continuing the previous conversation. I glanced her way. "I don't feel comfortable discussing the problems we had with your father, in front of you. No matter how we feel about him, he is your father and you love him. I don't want to disrespect you by talking about him in an unkind way." She smiled sweetly and said "That's okay, I'm alright with it."

With a cautious look at her I said "We were so excited to move here. We really liked your Dad at first. We planned to have your family over for a big barbeque when we got settled. We don't understand why things went so south, so fast. He didn't keep his word on anything and had no conscience or remorse what so ever for what he was doing to us."

Her husband chimed in. "He was looking forward to both of you as neighbors too. Maybe it can be like that again." I felt a slight uncontrollable glare fall over my eyes. "No. There has been too much damage. He has given us too many reasons not to ever trust him again. What he did isn't something we can forgive and forget and go on with life as friendly neighbors. He got everything he wanted and we're just supposed to forget about it? I really don't feel right talking any further about this."

Without a second of silence he said "We have come four hundred and fifty miles to make things right. Can we talk to your husband and you today and sort this out?"

The thoughts in my mind and heart were running wild. Why did this happen that day of all days? We were less than two hours away from our first open house guests arriving.

I still had cleaning to do. It was Saturday. No chance in contacting our lawyer.

He was supposed to get ahold of her if he wanted to settle. Why didn't he call her instead?

Did he find out from face book about the open house and was this an attempt to throw a wrench in it? Did he purposely show up on a Saturday knowing we wouldn't be able to contact our lawyer? Was he smart enough to figure all this out and maliciously plan his trip?

Why would he, his wife and two Amish minister's travel 450 miles to our house not even knowing if we'd be home?

With a matter of fact voice I said "Dan is working until noon. When he gets home, we have plans for the day. We won't be available until around 7 tonight." With a look of disappointment he replied "Well, the Ministers wanted to turn around and go home today but I will talk with them and see what they think about staying the night so that we can talk this evening. I will let you know."

He took a piece of paper out from the pocket of his shirt and scrawled his cell phone number on it, handing it to me. "If they will not stay, maybe we can do this over the phone."

With that, he and his wife said their goodbyes and made their way to the waiting van. I watched them drive down the road and into the driveway of the Bishops house as I shut our front door.

I picked up the phone and called Dan at work, telling him what was going on. Peace had escaped me. I was at the peak of my stress level and I rambled on and on about not being ready for the open house, the unexpected sellers visit and his extreme dishonesty. Dan assured me everything would be okay and he would be home soon to help me clean.

"I have to go, some one's knocking. I'll see you when you get home. Love you." I said as I hung up the phone.

The seller of our farm had quickly returned, walking from his Father-in-laws house just a short distance away. I opened the door. "The Ministers have agreed to stay. We will be back at 7:00." Putting on a false face of calmness I confirmed the time would work for us.

I couldn't help myself. "You know, that was a really nasty letter you wrote to us about the settlement. It was just plain mean and I'm still upset about it."

Without anyone with him this time to watch his actions, his cocky demeanor came out in full force. "I apologize but I was mad." His sternness in speaking told me he wasn't truly sorry at all.

There was a thick haze of contempt in the air between us. There may have been no one there to hear either one of us but I heard myself and to me, that's what mattered.

For that first five minutes we interacted with each other on that second visit, we had shown each other who we really were inside. The difference was, I could sleep at night with a clean heart and clear mind. I did continue to keep my peace but I had trouble holding in comments that were more like questions.

"A day before we were supposed to close, the Bishop kept calling us and we didn't answer the phone. The next thing we knew we were being black mailed for the fence panels and shelves. The real estate company told us the Bishop said that if we didn't write a statement saying we did not want the panels and shelves, the sale would be stopped."

With a glare he responded. "That's not true. I told the real estate company I would pay for half of the cost of the fence panels. They agreed to pay for the other half. When it came down to it they backed out."

My face was getting hot.

Why on earth would the real estate company agree to pay for half of the fence panels? What sense did that make? What about the shelves? We got back mailed for them too, did the real estate company agree to pay for half of them and then back out on that too? And the sheep. We had to write that we did not want the sheep. We begged for them to remove the sheep for months because they were destroying the barn. They made us write a statement saying we did not want them?

It was clear to us who was behind it all. The same man who said to Dan "Wouldn't it be awful if you put all that time and money into this place and then the seller backed out?" The crooked Bishop, in cahoots with his crooked Son-in-law.

I saw such ugliness in such a handsome young man. Dishonesty clung to him like a heavy fog as he talked to me from a lowered head with no eye contact, spewing useless words that were lighting flames inside me. I was losing my battle with holding my tongue but I was able to hang onto a calm voice.

"Didn't you read the contract? Those fence panels, the fence that was ripped out and the shelves were all supposed to come with this place. We're paying for them and we don't have them." He casually looked up at me and excused my comment by saying "Well, I don't really know how to read or understand contracts."

27

Our attorney had asked us to keep discussions to a minimum. He was supposed to contact her and only her, with settlement correspondence. I knew I needed to heed her advice. We had a few hours to decide what to do before the Ministers and he came back. It was time to end the conversation. "See you at seven" I said, as I closed the door behind me.

I had things to do but the first priority was for me to calm myself down. I made myself a fresh pot of coffee and sat down with a cup at my computer, not resisting to make a short post on face book about what had happened. The people on face book who had been following our story from the start where people God brought into our lives when we needed them. They were our support system. Our cheer leaders. They cared. Their opinions mattered to us.

Their responses where overwhelming. "Don't do it without a lawyer" "Tape or video record it" "Call your attorney" I read each post and as I took them into consideration, I swayed further and further from a talk with the Ministers and sellers that night.

Dan came home shortly after and made a b-line straight to me for a hug. We discussed the situation as he cracked a beer and helped me to hurry and finish the house work. I told him the opinions on face book were overwhelmingly against the meeting.

The floor in the living room was still wet from mopping when our first guests arrived.

It was Dan's Aunt Pat and Uncle Herv, closely followed by friends of my folks, Ed and Avis. There was that God thing working again. Bringing me the people I needed for strength right when I needed them. Being around Ed and Avis always made me feel grounded. Cared about. Loved. Made me remember who I was. An Emerson. A Pascoe. The hug I got from Avis that day was sent from my Mother, I was sure of it. Having them there at that moment was what I needed.

Although I had only known them for a few years, Pat and Herv gave me a similar feeling. That comforting feeling that said no matter what, everything will be alright.

The older generation that came from before cell phones and fast paces are gems to our society. They are the wise. The connected. The truly honest without motives kind of folks. They don't create problems or drama. They sooth those things. They parent those things with an open hearted logic you don't see much of anymore.

The six of us sat at the table and talked about the pending "meeting." Someone said "They could be trying to blackmail you to stop the sale of the book." Another said "Two Amish ministers, the seller and his wife's word against just you and Dan. What side do you think the Amish Ministers would take if they turned around and said you blackmailed them? Who knows what they're up to? If I were you, I wouldn't do it. Not a good idea."

I looked across the table at Dan. "I think it would be a good idea to call the seller and tell him we have reconsidered our decision to meet with them tonight and he needs to contact our lawyer to settle. If we call now to tell them, they can head back home to Ohio as they had originally planned." Dan agreed, as did our guests.

I got up from the table and walked to the hutch in the dining room to retrieve the sellers' number. In a matter of minutes Dan was on the phone. "Hi, this is Dan Wood. Lori and I have decided meeting isn't a good idea. We need you to contact our lawyer to settle. Have a good night."

It felt like a load lifted. The rest of the day went well. Our open house was a success and although not many took a tour of the house to check it out, we did get several people who simply wanted to sit and talk. We loved that. The day had turned out okay after all. As time wound down and as the end of the open house was nearing, we felt good. It was well past six. Time to wind down and reflect on the day.

"Lori, what color van were they in?" I said "Maroon, why?" I looked out to the side drive and there they were, pulling in. "Oh no" I said. "Must be they didn't get our message." Dan got up from his chair and said he'd take care of it.

I stayed behind. I had enough of this drama earlier that morning. Seeing that van there in the drive way felt like the on button had just been pushed again.

I watched Dan walk to the van as the seller and his wife got out and approached him. I went to my art room to escape what was going on. I knew if the seller was to start his dishonesty with Dan, things may not go well.

Shortly after, I heard the kitchen door open and shut. Dan was back. I emerged from the art room. "How'd it go?" Dan shook his head.

"Well, I felt kind of bad because his wife was smiling and when I told them they had to contact our layer she looked devastated and said, but we have money! He started to talk about the contract and things and I just cut him off and told him he needs to call our lawyer. He said they drove 450 miles just to settle and I told him he should have called first. He said he didn't have our number."

My response to Dan was "Hello? He has our address, he used to live here. He could have sent us a letter giving us a heads up. As far as our number, I can think of two Amish folks here who have it. He could have called one of them and asked. There's no excuse for not letting us know they were coming. Did he say he was going to call our lawyer?"

Dan said "Yes, he said if that's what he had to do to settle and make things right, he would do that. He said it a few times."

There were so many things I was unsure of but there was one thing I was sure of. A second book. The knock at the door that morning confirmed it. It was a chance for the Bishop and seller to redeem themselves of what they did.

I would give them that chance to take responsibility for what happened and turn things around for themselves, for their community and for being the bad apples who sometimes give good people a bad name.

They could fix this and I would put it right there in print and we could all live happily ever after. Yes, I would be writing a second book.

I sat down and emailed a letter to our lawyer that night explaining the situation. The email subject was "Head's up!" I was sure if they had traveled 450 miles just to settle and said they would contact our lawyer if that's what they had to do, they would. I wanted to let her know she would be hearing from them soon.

Less than a week later we were informed by a friend that the seller came here to go to a wedding. He had been here since the previous Thursday.

Our House.

4
Canine Show Down

Any day, the seller would contact our lawyer offering to settle and we could use the money to help dig ourselves out from under the hole we were thrown. We could buy new fence panels. They would come in so useful for sectioning the pasture off for the horses. We could put some on the principal of the loan.

We were hopeful that things were finally going to be made right. We even let ourselves get a little excited.

We believed the seller really was forced to come to us to make things right. That didn't matter to us. What mattered was that he was being held accountable. The Amish in Ohio weren't turning the other cheek on what happened. It seemed the seller was like a child who had broken a window, being dragged by the nape of the neck by his parents to apologize and pay restitution. Admirable to their culture, to keep the bad apples in line.

We would be patient and wait and I would try to shake off the conversations I had with the seller on the day of the open house. Thinking about his attitude and dishonesty only frustrated me and left me feeling angry. I had to remind myself not to let it drag me down. There were so many good people in our world to focus on who were much more worth my thoughts.

There were so many new memories to make and they were being made fast at the farm. God was blessing us with peace and laughter.

Now and then we would walk to the pond with Roxy in tow. Being a black lab we were sure sooner or later she would love the water. She loved playing fetch.

"Hey Dan, throw a stick in and see if she'll get it." I said. Dan went to the nearest apple tree and broke of a branch, tossing it into the middle of the pond.

Roxy was off like a bullet belly smacking into the water. Her first swim. The uncertainty in her eyes showed as she struggled through the water to get the stick. Her head above water and her body directly below she was paddling for her life. A black bobber. Head in the air, nose pointed to the sky, paws flailing, she was going nowhere. Suddenly she went under. "She's gonna drown!" Dan said. I assured him she would be okay. "She's a lab, you need to just let her figure it out." Roxy continued to struggle.

"I have to save her!" Dan said has he took off his boots. Within seconds he was in the pond up to his chest in water. He gathered Roxy in his arms and guided her back to land, walking out of the water. A sloshing sound with every step.

On the bank of the pond I was bent over laughing so hard my cheeks hurt.

On the way back to the house with both a wet dog and a wet husband I smiled and declared "This is how memories are made."

By then it was early July. Traffic past our farm had suddenly slowed down. The post that marked the name of our road below our farm seemed to be sheared in half and the green sign laid in the tall grass. Someone with a GPS who came to buy a book told us the sign at the top of the road above the farm was gone as well. Dan and I took a walk to check it out. He suspected it had been ripped from the post.

More and more stories were surfacing about the Bishops crooked ways and small town rumors were flying. "I heard he's moving to Wisconsin" "I heard he's moving and his son is going to take over his business." "I heard they aren't having the auction at his farm this year."

The rumors had started the previous fall with the onset of the infamous face book page but we had seen no change in the neighborhood as far as the Bishop was concerned. He was still there. We were going about our business and he was going about his. Well that is, until there was somewhat of an unfortunate event one day.

Our dog Deja is a Siberian husky. A beautiful dog with a thick gray coat, white mask and deep brown eyes. When she isn't inside lounging on the floor or playing tug-o-war with her side kick Roxy, we kept her on a chain outside. She tended to have a mind of her own at times and if she decided go off from the property alone to take a stroll in the woods, there was no question in my mind she would pass for a coyote. A visible coyote in the daylight wouldn't last long in these parts.

Now and then we would let her off her chain to walk to the pond with us. By then Roxy had learned to swim and enjoyed endless games of fetch the stick from the middle of the pond while Deja relished the smells and sounds of the pasture and surrounding woods.

When she would start to stray, Dan's deep commanding voice would bring her back. My voice did nothing.

There was an occasion when Dan decided to take her to the garage with him and Roxy while he did some work. I was always against this, as Deja had no sense when it came to vehicles and the shop was close to the road.

My concerns were heightened by memories of her beloved half Brother being struck and killed by a truck. As with situations of this sort, I put it in God's hands and went to my art room to work. I tried to put it out of my head.

Lots of buggies went by every day. Most of the time I'd glance up from my work and out that window to the left of me and that day was no different. I saw the Bishop in his cart. That instrumental Wizard of Oz song clicked into gear in my mind.

What I saw behind that buggy snapped me to and put a sudden screech to the music playing in my head. His little jack Russell terrier was trailing behind him.

The Jack had been at our house several times since we had moved in, when Deja had been out on her chain. He would bounce and play just out of her reach. He'd run through the lawn, to the garage and barn while she ached to protect her territory, panting and whining.

Now he was headed up the road, past the garage. Directly in sight of a free, unleashed Siberian husky with a good memory. I sat tight in my chair not wanting to know what was going to happen. Dan would take care of it. But what if he was busy and preoccupied? What if he was running something loud and couldn't hear anything?

Deja would listen to him if she misbehaved, right?

There were too many questions. I had to go look to see what was going on. Off to the kitchen window I went. Oh no. Not good. What I expected would happen, did. Dan was standing in the road trying to get ahold of Deja's collar.

The jack Russell was standing up to her, egging her on as she picked him up and shook him. Dan was yelling at Deja and the Bishop was yelling at the jack Russell, the whole while never stopping his buggy. Dan got Deja by the collar and the Jack Russell ran to catch up with the Bishops buggy.

Dan brought her back to the house and put her back on her chain. "Is the jack Russell ok? I asked as I inspected Deja's fur and mouth area for blood. There was no blood to be found. "Yes, he's fine. That's the end of that. I guess I won't let Deja loose to hang out with me anymore." He said as he tried to catch his breath. "But that dog deserved it!"

The Bishops Dog

Deja

5
Hay

In early spring we met an Amish gentleman who was interested in planting oats in a back part of the property. An area that wasn't pastured, near the woods. Overgrown with golden rod and picker bushes, it wouldn't be much good unless it was dug up and taken care of.

Planting oats there sounded like a good idea to get rid of the Jing weeds and to tame the land.

He was also interested in cutting and baling our hay fields. We talked about working out a deal with him as far as splitting the hay, maybe even helping him to hay with our tractor.

The options were many and things were left in the air to think about. Planting season was approaching. He would get back to us in the next couple weeks and we could talk more and make a decision. Time went on and weeks went by. We didn't hear back from him. We were unsure why and could only speculate.

Dan's truck had broken down early on in the spring and had been sitting in the driveway waiting until we had the money to fix it. Haying season as coming as well as fair time. We weren't so sure how much longer my S-10 would last as far as a way for Dan to get to work. We needed his diesel to haul hay and take my daughters horses to the fair. It was time to think about repairing his truck. Off it went to a diesel mechanic.

Summer came and we knew it would soon escape us. We needed to think about food for our horses and goats for the winter. Assuming the Amish gentleman had changed his mind, we made a deal with a local English farmer to hay our fields. He would do the work and we would supply baling twine and such, here and there. We would get the hay from the smaller field. He would take the hay from the large field.

With two cuttings there would be more than enough for everyone.

Within a week of talking to the farmer, our Amish friend who was interested in cutting our fields stopped by. Although he seemed disappointed, he understood he was a day late and a dollar short. There were no hard feelings.

It was haying made simple for us. With the use of Dan's tractor and their hay wagon, Dan, Morgan, Kyle and I were out in the field picking up bales and stacking them onto the wagon. It was a short drive to the barn, where they would be put away for snowy weather. It was family time. It was fun time.

Haying season was always time to show those boys what we country girls were made of. It was a time to take all the dogs to the field with us and let them run, play and ride in the back of my pick up on trips back and forth to the barn. An occasional stop to remove a sliver. An occasional laugh at Dan or me for grunting while tossing a bale of hay.

In the larger field below us the farmer and his group of hard working friends and family where doing the same with two hay wagons. Bales of hay were spread the lengths of both of the fields.

Trucks, tractors, hay wagons and people working hard. Making memories. Preparing for the coming months.

"Dan, can I drive the tractor while you guys throw the bales?" Morgan asked.

She was very much a tomboy. Just like her momma but with an edge. Dan smiled. "Yes, you can." He may as well have said "I thought you'd never ask." I can remember that smile on his face as he showed her how things worked and we all laughed at how she had to stand up to see where she was going. On the back of the wagon I quickly learned to hang on tight for sudden stops and starts.

After one fully stacked trailer load I started to make my way through the field to my truck with the dogs trailing behind me. It was parked near the road. Expecting Morgan to follow as well, I heard "Hey, can I ride up there on top of the hay?" Before any words could escape my lips, Dan replied back. "Get up there."

I saw the danger of the situation and thoughts of the hay toppling over on the way home struck panic inside me. I didn't watch her climb up onto that mound of stacked hay. I didn't watch them leave the field and come down the road. I walked to my truck, got in and went to the house to wait. It was times like this that I had to remember to put things in God's hands. It was times like this when I remembered that I always felt like my parents worried too much about me. It was times like this that I understood why.

Her Brother and she are my babies. It would never matter how old they were. Worrying would never go away.

I used to think that no matter how old I was, my parents could always make me feel like I was twelve. Now I understood why. Parenting never really ends when there is so much love involved.

Replacing that worry with letting things rest in God's hands was what had to be done in most situations to keep peace within myself.

While in the house I grabbed my camera. The tractor and trailer with Morgan on top of the hay would be pulling in soon. I made my way to the side door to see. There it was. She was safe and sound and helping to direct Dan as he backed the tractor and the wagons load into the barn. I pulled the camera strap from around my neck and yelled to her to do a beauty queen wave from her "float." Her small frame, long blonde ponytail and bright smile took over the camera from atop the hay as she flattened her hand out and turned it from side to side.

In a quick second she was back to directing Dan, ducking to keep from hitting her head on the entrance to the barn.

Life felt so good. So many things were falling into place. The right people started to come into our lives at the right times. Not a night went past that I wasn't thanking God for everything he brought to us.

Karma seemed to be coming around for us and each time it did, it was duly noticed. There were still road blocks and speed bumps in our lives and not everything was perfect but that was life. After the previous summer anything that went wrong could not compare to what we faced back then.

This winter would be different. There would be no hauling hay in two feet of snow in twenty degree weather. No hauling twenty bales at a time from ten miles away to keep the horses fed. All of our hay for the winter would be here, tucked away in the mow of the barn.

The pasture had been cleaned up and fixed and Dan had built a door in the mow that would allow me to throw the hay from the window. The water could be run a short distance to the horses and goats through a hose. No more carrying bale by bale and five gallon water buckets the length of the barn and up a hill every morning and night. No more falling in the ice and snow.

That hard winter was behind us and the summer seemed to be fading fast but without a moment of it wasted or taken for granted. As we did land clean up and worked around the farm, I enjoyed watching the horses in the warm sunshine as they roamed the new pasture, exploring the pond and woods.

Our old gelding and herd boss, Tyke, was in his glory as he guided his mares to new territory. Although blanketed on cold and snowy days and put inside nights, he still looked frail from a hard winter and old age, but that boy ran and bucked and kicked like a young stud. I hoped that soon the lush pasture and apple orchard would help to rebuild his weight before winter came again.

Now and then I couldn't help myself but to set work aside and go out into the pasture just to be with him.

My loud clapping hands always brought him running to me. He was the first horse I had owned in over twenty years.

A gentle giant. A tall Appaloosa with a copper colored coat and a spotted white blanket on his rear end. Big, soft, kind eyes and a loyal heart. My instincts and horse sense trusted him to take care of Morgan who at the time of his purchase, had no riding experience.

Over the years he and she did St. Jude rides, organized trail rides, parades and he even went to school with her one day for a class project. To her, he was the door that opened to her dreams.

I felt like Tyke had helped me raise that girl and had helped her to get through some rough times. Me too.

You see, before I met Dan I didn't think I needed anyone. Didn't want anyone. When I felt lonely or sad, time with Tyke helped to put me at peace. When I was upset I'd saddle him up and fly down that dirt road pretending my troubles where being left in the dust. "Riding Wildfire, we're gonna ride him. Gonna leave our troubles behind...."

Shortly after I met Dan, it was time to retire Tyke. He was showing signs of age and it was time for him to live out his life being pampered and spoiled. No more trail rides.

The last time I rode him was when I jumped on his back to ride him to the barn. Back at our old place. He looked sleepy. Calm. Why not? No bridle. No saddle. No halter. I took off my flannel shirt and wrapped it around his thick neck, leading him to a tree that had fallen over to attempt to get on his back. With more than a few tries, I made it!

Once on his back his old tired eyes seemed to get a sparkle and we quickly made our way through the trees and to the stream. I felt his body gather under him and knew it wasn't going to be good. I clenched his mane and held on as tight as my legs would hold to his barrel as we made our landing. He wasn't done. He continued a fast paced trot with crow hops every other step. From his back it felt like a full blown buck as I held on around his neck until I felt a chance to voluntarily dismount.

Whew, landed on my feet, laughing.

"MOM, what did you do that for??!! You can't ride Tyke like that, he gets crazy!" I heard Morgan yell. Still catching my breath as I started to laugh I replied "Now you tell me." He was old. I was old. But for just a few seconds he and I were both young again.

Now there he was, out in the pasture. Holding so many memories. Still bossing those mares. Still looking noble and wise. Still bringing so much peace. Still being my friend and sharing in our happily ever after.

Morgan on her float

6
Worthless Words

We were outside every chance we had, raking, shoveling and piling up junk. Trips to the land fill. Trips to the burn pile that was quickly growing again and awaiting a wet burning day.

When that day came Dan stood there most of the time feeding it. He had been cleaning his garage and there was much saw dust and tiny pieces of broken boards. At first he tried to pick the nails and screws out of the saw dust but after collecting a wheel barrow full of them he gave up. It was a losing battle. It was decided that he would wait till it burnt down and rake it. It was away from any place the animals would be.

Early evening his cousin Rodney and his girlfriend Kim stopped by. What a nice surprise! We all ended up standing by the fire on that warm July night. I went to the house and grabbed some lawn chairs and beers. Laughter, a big fire, a starry night and a few beers. What's better than that? Chicken. Yes, chicken. We had four halves in the fridge and a grill waiting for them. Tuna fish salad already made and in the fridge. Dan and I decided to walk to the house and get the grill going. It was dark away from the fire but by then we knew our way to the house.

Once there, we saw headlights stopped on the road by the fire. We wondered who it could be. Maybe a friend who saw the fire and wanted to drop in? No, the truck was leaving. We would ask our guests who it was.

"Who stopped by?" Dan asked. Rod and Kim both said they didn't know who it was. "Some young kid who stopped to ask if this was where the Amish party was." They thought he had been drinking. They went on to tell us the name of the person's home he was trying to find.

Dan and I looked at each other. Wait, what? No way. He was looking for the Bishops house. They didn't know who the Bishop was or where he lived, so they couldn't help him.

A memorable night. A nice break from tiring work. We sat at the fire until late and ate chicken halves and tuna fish salad at 1 AM.

After several weeks at the shop, Dan got a call his truck was done. We jumped in the car and with cash in hand from his profit sharing check to pay the bill, we headed to get his truck.

An expensive trip but this would mean he had it back. Just in the nick of time before fair. We were all smiles as he headed out of the shops driveway. I would follow him home in my car.

Dan was moving about 15 miles an hour and black smoke started billowing from his truck. Enough smoke to make me pull over to regain my sight of the road. Within a quarter mile from the shop we were turning around and going back. Immensely disappointed, we had to leave the truck there for further repairs. We didn't have it in time for haying. Now we wouldn't have it in time for fair either.

Two weeks had passed with no word from the seller to our attorney. It was still early. He gave his word to Dan several times that he would contact her to settle with us.

Giving your word between men in both the Amish and English world meant something. At least it did at one time. The world was changing. People were changing.

The Bishop gave us his word on several occasions that previous summer. His word was worthless.

Would the seller's word be worthless as well? We couldn't imagine that in such a serious situation as this, with others involved in knowing what was going on.

The secrets were out to the Amish in Ohio as to the dirty pool he and his father-in-law played when selling us this farm. They would be made to make things right. The seller would be made to keep his word. We were sure it would happen. All we had to do is keep living. Keep working hard. Keep thanking God not for what we didn't have but for what we did have.

We needed to keep patience and keep peace inside of us while we waited to see what would happen. Always positive thoughts. See the best in people. Just keep living and let life happen Treasure even the little things that make life an adventure along the way. Little dogs included.

One mid-July afternoon I heard barking. It had been raining and windy and the windows to my art room were shut. It went on and on. Did one of the neighbors get a new dog?

It sounded like some sort of hound dog. It would yelp, bark and whimper for a while and then go silent. Like a lonely dog on a short leash. It wasn't uncommon to hear in the summer time with the windows open but normally the sound silenced for good sooner or later.

Early that evening I said to Dan "I keep hearing a dog. I've heard it on and off all day. I went out into the pasture earlier to check. The barking stopped and I didn't see anything." By now the rain was coming down in buckets and there was a chill in the air that seemed to prompt the dog into a continuous bark. Dan came to my art room to listen. "Sounds like it's out in the pasture."

Dan put on his rain coat and grabbed the flash light from atop the refrigerator. I slipped on a jacket and my barn boots. By the time I got outdoors to catch up with him, he had already found the source of the noise.

There was a very small goat wire pasture built inside the big pasture right behind our home. It's size and that there is no way in or out of it has always been a mystery to us. With no access for the horses to gain entrance, the grass was waist high.

Dan had bent the wire enough to step over the goat fence and he was kneeling down, pushing the tall wet grass to the ground with his hands. "Oh you poor little thing." He said. When he stood up he had a shivering little beagle in his arms. He tucked her into his rain coat and made his way back over the fence.

"When I found her she stopped barking and rolled over on her back. She acted scared. She must have got in here somehow and couldn't get back out."

We took her inside and dried her off with bath towels and paper towels. She looked so scared and was still shaking but so happy to be found. Whose was she?

I remembered seeing an Amish couple walking their dogs earlier that year. The collars on their dogs where different from what I had ever seen. They were a bright orange plastic. This little girl had that sort of collar.

"I wonder if she's the Bishops." I said. "I know he had an ad to sell a beagle, tacked up at Reeds not too long ago but it's not there anymore. If it was his it seems like his kids would have heard her and came to get her. The kids know we are okay with them and they are welcome here. Maybe he wouldn't let them come get her though."

Dan looked disgruntled. "No, I don't think she is his." From looking at him holding the still damp little dog I could tell he was already hoping we didn't find the owner. "She has to belong to someone. Let's take a run up the road to our Amish friend's house and see if they know who she belongs to." I said.

It was nearing dark when Dan knocked on their door. The dog stayed in the S-10 with me and was anxious and panting. It was obvious this was her first ride in a vehicle. Within moments Dan was walking toward the truck. Once inside, he turned to me. "I feel bad, I woke them up. They said they don't know whose dog it is." "I still think she might be the Bishops dog." I replied.

We drove back to the house in silence and pulled into the drive way to park. The sky was dimly lit through the falling night and the rain had slowed down to a sprinkle. Dan got out of the truck with the beagle in his arms and turned to me. "I'm going to put her down and walk until I almost get to the Bishops house and then I'm going to turn around and come back. If she follows me home, she isn't his." I agreed that was a good idea and watched them walk off into the summer night and then went inside to wait for his return, with or without his new friend.

Not long after I heard the door open. I went to the kitchen to greet Dan. He was alone. "Well, she followed me and when we got there it was weird. She looked at the house and looked at me like she was saying goodbye and then went up to the corner of the yard and ran to the house." I smiled. "That's her home. I'll bet she missed those kids and I'll bet they missed her right back."

7
The Auction

Dan called me during the day when he was at work to see how things were here at the farm. To make sure the animals and I are okay. To see if I need him to pick anything up on his way home.

On one such call he said "Guess what I heard today? I heard the auction isn't at the Bishops house this year." My answer was a calm "Really?"

Amish Above the law had been published in June and it didn't take long for rumors to fly. It would have surprised me if this new rumor was true. The annual auction for the Amish school house, as far as I knew, had always been at the Bishops home.

I took it with a grain of salt and for the next week or two I did a regular check online to see if I could find out any auction information. Then there it was. An online ad for the auction. It said "7th Annual Auction. Held at a new location this year!"

Although it benefited the same Amish community schools, the new location was a couple miles away, in another township. Far away from the Bishops home.

This was the first year there was no mention of his name in the online advertisement.

Not long after, our farrier came to take care of our horses' feet. He was one of the contacts for the auction. I had known him for years and always considered him, Amish or not, to be one of the good guys.

Many times when talking with Amish men, women are made to feel beneath them. Like what we say doesn't matter. In English terms, some Amish men have a chauvinistic personality.

Our farrier wasn't like that at all. Never had been. He was compassionate and caring and listened rather you were male or female. I got to know two of his sons. One came with him to help with the horses and the other trained my horse, Blessing, a few years back.

Both nice boys that grew into good men like their father. I told the farrier I would like to donate a piece of artwork to the auction to do my part in helping their schools. A gesture of good will. When he asked how much I wanted for commission I said "oh no, I just want to donate. I don't want any money for it."

I donate my art work often to charities. My choice are charities close to my heart. Children, cancer patients, animal shelters. God gave me talent in my right hand that I am thankful for. It helps pay the bills. There's nothing left afterward and yet there is so much.

There is something I can give that can bring a smile without being out a dime. Something simple. My time and Gods guidance through my eyes and hands.

We decided it would work out easier to take my donation to the Bishops son, or another member of the auction committee, who both live right down the road, rather than to make a trip to the farriers' home.

I painted an Amish scene on a metal sap bucket that was left behind here at the farm in the mounds of debris.

As I drove down the road and into the Bishops sons' driveway I saw several tiny young girls playing in the back yard. They were having a tea party outside a beautifully built Amish play house. I opened the car door and got out with the bucket in my arms. The children started to walk to the house. The smallest child had a cat swaddled in a blanket carrying it like a baby doll.

Inside my soul was melting like butter at the sweetness of what I saw. I smiled and waved, knowing at that age they wouldn't understand English.

Before the children made it to the house to alert their Mother to my visit, the back door opened exposing a young woman with an uncertain and maybe even a little stern look on her face. She was surely the Bishops Daughter-in-law.

"Hi, I'm Lori, from up the road. I brought this painting for the auction. I was told I could drop it off here. I don't want any money for it, I just want to donate it." Her face softened.

"You painted this? This is very nice, thank you." I told her I was happy to help. With a little small talk I was on my way back to my car, both of us smiling as we said our goodbyes.

With every new Amish person I met a voice inside me questioned a reaction to the book. I wanted the Amish community to read it. Rather related to the Bishop or not, I wanted them to know our side. We needed them to understand what really happened and that they were being blamed for things they didn't do.

The book had been out a little over a month and I had done two book signings. The next signing would be at my friend Kathie's boutique. I was excited. Her store was in a bigger town than what was in my area and we had a lot of face book followers there that I hoped would come. The book signing was coming up in a couple short weeks. It was time to place an ad in the newspaper.

"Amish Above the Law" Non-fiction, authored by former Wellsville resident Lori (Mills) Wood. Book signing August 13 from 6-8:00 PM at Karisma Boutique. Books are available on Amazon and at Karisma."

A week after placing the ad, I picked up the paper and scanned its pages. There is was, top left hand corner. I was content in knowing the ad made it in time and was about to close the paper when I noticed something. A quarter page size ad on the same page but on the lower right side of the paper.

An ad for the annual Amish auction, complete with "At a different location this year." I thought to myself "How ironic is that?"

I advertised the auction on face book, giving directions to the new location when people asked. The auction was an important part of the Amish communities fund raising for their school house. Were we the reason the auction had a new location?

When it came right down to it our thoughts were yes and no. The public would come to an Amish auction but not if it was hosted at the Bishops home. It was clear to us, because we told our story and he had been exposed, the auction had been moved away from the Bishops farm.

8
Angel in Cats Clothing

The third week in August the hill came alive with the buzzing of busy Amish preparing for the auction. Powerful golden Belgians with wagon loads of items on their way to the new location were abundant. Bare foot women and children walked the dirt road to the new auction site.

Everyone was dressed in their Sunday best and excited about the annual event. Including a dressed to the Amish nines, very handsome Aden Troyer. He was here to help with the auction and stopped to pay me a visit to order some more art work I could ship to him at a later date. We had a brief conversation and I gave him a complimentary book. It was good to hear he was happy and doing well.

That weekend for me brought back painful memories of my Mothers passing. A year had gone by so fast. Prayer helped me to push away the sad memories and replace them with mental images of my Mother in happier times. One of those special memories had been heavy on my mind for the past year.

It was the summer of 2010. The last year that everything felt normal and the days passed without much care. Life was all about going through the motions. There were trail rides and family gatherings. Picnics and barbeques. Life was good.

That June, I came around the corner of the garage and saw a flash of black and white as I made my way up the sidewalk. I looked at the back step to the sliding glass door and I noticed a can of cat food. As I looked up, I saw my father sitting at his usual place at the table in the sun room. Opening the door I smiled.

"Dad, you're feeding a cat?" He never cared for cats. He smirked "I'm just trying to get it close enough to kick it."

I looked out into the lawn and saw her cowering by his tomato plants. She was mangy looking. Long haired and dirty. I stepped back outside and slowly started to approach her. She ran off into the creek behind the house.

My Dad smiled. His response to what he saw seemed so unusual. "She'll come around. I want your Mother to have that cat."

I often made visits to my parent's home and each time I saw the stray I tried to befriend her. Slowly. Cautiously. I'd sit on the sidewalk and wait for her trust, until one day, she approached me. I was able to give her a short, unthreatening pet before she scampered off and into the creek bed.

Each visit with her got better until one day, she allowed me to pick her up. From through the screen door I heard my dad say "Look, Nancy, Lori picked up the cat." He was beaming with a look that said "I knew she could do it." I heard my Mother laugh. "Lori, you're the cat whisperer."

Summer turned to fall and the cat had made her way now and then, to the step to eat. She never stayed long, always nervous and alert to any strange noise or person approaching.

By the time my father fell ill, although she stayed outside most of the time, she called my parents place home. The night before my Fathers passing, she came inside and jumped onto his hospital bed. As timid as she was it was that strange move from her that caught me off guard.

I now knew why he said "I want your Mother to have that cat." She would be there for Mom to take care of. To love. To help fill those painful nights alone. So that there would be life inside that house.

I made an appointment to get the cat spayed and to get her shots. I got a litter box and promised I'd be I charge of cleaning it. She earned her way into my Mothers broken heart little by little as she perched on the arm of my Mothers chair while she watched her favorite TV shows. As she greeted my Mother every morning at the sliding glass door. As she gently put her paws on my Mothers knee for attention.

"Lori, do you know where that cat slept last night? She slept at the end of your father's side of the bed." The once stray, long haired dirty cat, skittish of everyone but my Mother, was an angel in disguise. My Mother named her "Princess."

Shortly before my Mother fell ill, Princess got fleas and the house was infested. She had to stay outside. Mom was admitted to the hospital and diagnosed with Cancer. Tearfully, in that hospital room I promised her that if I could find Princess and catch her, I would take her to the farm to live with us. Princess wasn't seen again, until the night of my Mothers passing.

As I stood outside my Mother's house looking at that stunning sky, softly and sadly singing "Beyond the Sunset" to myself I saw Princess in the distance on a grassy bank by the pond my Dad so loved. She was just sitting there. Watching. I moved toward her wanting so bad to pick her up and just hold her. She quickly scampered off into the nearby trees and vanished.

Disheartened, I took the brush Princess loved so much to be brushed with, home with me. I took that silly little bowl my Mother used to use to scoop cat food from a large plastic container and I took the plastic container, too.

I asked Morgan, who lived a stone's throw from my Mother's home, to keep an eye out for the cat and then I put it in God's hands.

Over a year had passed with no signs or sightings of Princess. Someone set a live trap in hopes to catch her for me the previous fall and they did in fact catch a black and white cat. It wasn't Princess.

I was sure she hadn't survived the winter. I was sure she had fallen victim to a predator or vehicle. Hope was lost that I would ever see her again. In my mind I conceded that maybe this was what was meant to be. I had to accept Gods plans for Princess.

The auction was over and the following week went by like any other. I didn't understand what was happening with me when it came to thinking about losing my parents. I stopped crying. I stopped thinking. I felt blank. When a hint of that heartache of loss started to appear it would just vanish. A mental block would take over. I wondered what was wrong with me. I needed to cry. Why couldn't I just cry? And then one night I did.

Roxy started to bark. It was 10:30 at night. Who could be here this late? My mind raced. Were the kids alright? What was going on? I heard Morgan's voice and felt a sigh of relief. What was she doing here at this hour?

As she made her way to my art room I heard a meow. I knew. I just knew. She was carrying a dusty blue cat carrier and as she entered the room, she sat it on the floor and smiled. I felt a lump in my throat. Overwhelmed with emotion I dropped to my knees and put my head in my hands. I began to sob uncontrollably. Gaining my composure was difficult.

With tears still streaming, I opened the cat carrier and pulled Princess out, holding her close. She wasn't afraid. She was cuddling into me as much as I was to her. She remembered me. Morgan, watching with watery eyes, was in awe at the connection between the skittish feline and myself.

I stammered out the words "How? Where?" Tears by now where flowing down Morgan's face as she replied.

"Princess started to go to Mary Katherine's house. Mary Katherine left food outside for her. She knew the cat was Grandmas so she had her daughter tell me while I was working at the store."

Mary Katherine was a very dear friend of my Mothers. Her daughter Vicky was a childhood friend of mine and she had just started to work at Reeds Market, where Morgan works. Where had Princess been the past year? Of all of the homes to go to, how did she pick my Mothers dear friends home?

Princess had made her way to the farm. Delivered by the guidance of angels, she made her way to me. Mom knew I needed her. Many tears were shed in the following days as I looked into her big yellow eyes and held her close. As I fed her with that silly little bowl out of that big plastic container. As I brushed her with that brush she so loved to be brushed with. She became a part of Mom I could hug and love and at times I'd swear I'd smell Mom as I held that cat in my arms.

Still shy and timid, for a time she hid in my art room closet only coming out to eat or to get a drink. She would escape upstairs to get under a bed or in a closet if Dan was home or company came, reappearing at night when the house was quiet and still and then in my lap she would leap.

Before long it was apparent that she needed me as well. While on a kitchen run from my art room one evening, I stopped in my tracks at what I saw.

My Mothers recliner was in our living room. The very same recliner that she and Princess used to sit in. Mom in her chair, Princess beside her on its arm rest. They had shared hours and hours of TV and reading in that chair.

Princess was laying there against the arm rest with her head on the seat of the chair, looking as sad as a cat can look.

The chair has since become hers. She slept there every night. Some nights when it was late and I was on my way to bed, feeling sad or out of sorts, missing my folks, I'd stop at that chair and pick Princess up. I'd sit down and recline it.

And then we would just sit there together for a while. No lights, no sounds. From the darkness and quiet came peace.

In my heart I wondered how many times my Mother did the same after my father passed away. Was Princess brought to her to help ease her heartbreak? Was she part of a memory that my Mom held on to for comfort? Did she talk to her and hug her and look into those big yellow eyes and not feel so alone in her empty home?

I chose to think so.

Now here she was with me. Easing the pain of missing my Mother. Making me laugh in the same quirky ways she used to make my Mother laugh. Putting her front paws on my knee for a pet. Jumping into my lap for a brushing. Lightly tapping me in the face with her paw with no real explanation why. Yet still remaining a "one person cat." Afraid of almost everyone but me.

I prayed she would consider opening up to all the love she was missing out on. Time would tell.

The night I found Princess in my Mothers Chair

9
Reality

Dan got a call that his truck as ready for him. We had no money for the repair bill this time so the truck loan had to be refinanced to pay for it. We just couldn't seem to get ahead. Nothing seemed simple but we had the previous year to compare problems. Things could be worse. We could be back in 2012.

Dan started driving his truck back and forth to work and the S-10 was parked by the shop. The inspection had run out. Oh what memories that little truck held. I used it to drive Morgan back and forth to the bus stop when she was in school. It carried saddles and hay and flats of flowers.

It started when no one else's vehicles would start and was deemed "the dependable one" by Dan, even though he was a Ford fan.

Over the past year Dan had driven it instead of

his own to save gas on his trips to work. It had lived a full life in the five years I owned it. Now there it sat. It was no longer "my baby" "my pride and joy" my little truck had become in sorts, a man mobile. I took a broom, a garbage bag and bucket of soapy water to the spot the truck was parked and cleaned it out the best I could. I got it back to the condition I used to keep it in. It looked like "my baby" again. I would discuss with Dan on rather to sell it or not.

"Are you going to start driving my truck again soon?" I said one night at the table. "Why?" he replied.

"Well, it's just been sitting there doing nothing for a couple months and I'm paying insurance and registration on it. It needs work and I don't even think it'll pass PA inspection anyway. I want to sell it while I can if you're not going to drive it." Dan was adamant on keeping it.

"Okay, fine." I said. "If you are willing to fix it up enough so it's drivable, I can get it inspected and you start driving it again, I'll keep it."

He replied "No, it's your truck. Sell it if you want to."

I discovered it had a broken brake line while moving it from the spot he had last parked it. I ended up selling the truck, blown brake line and all, very cheap to someone who wanted parts and the motor from it to put a truck together for his Daughter.

Goodbye little S-10. You were good to us.

Little did we know at the time, that the decision made to sell it may have been saved Dan's life a couple months down the road.

A message on face book came shortly before Labor Day weekend. The lead character from the "Amish Mafia" TV show was in the area.

I thought it was a joke and then along came a picture. What was he doing here? It peaked my interest as messages came into our face book page with sightings. "He's at a bar drunk." "He got kicked out of bar for being drunk and trying to start a fight." "He is charging people $10 to get their picture taken with him."

Had he heard about what was going on here? Was this going to be some kind of publicity stunt? If it was, we would take no part in it.

With everything that had gone on the previous year it sure was hard not to be paranoid. For him to be in this area was interesting to say the least.

Rumors flew and then where put to rest. Our minds were eased when we learned he was only here to stay with friends over the holiday weekend. One thing was certain. He hung out with some of our face book followers. If he didn't know about our struggle with the Bishop and seller, he knew now.

I'd always had a problem with those Amish reality shows and had just previously talked with an Amish friend about them. I found that most Amish "Reality shows" have very little reality and it pains me that people who are intrigued with the Amish but have never been around them, may watch a show and form an opinion based on things that aren't true.

For example. Some shows tell of Amish rules and regulations when the truth is, those rules and regulations vary from community to community.

Some communities may be very strict and unforgiving, running a tight ship while others may be lax in comparison. To group them together as all one sect is just not fair.

I think my biggest peeve is when a TV camera shows a community as a dark and dank place. Drab music as the camera scans a plain house with no shutters or curtains. A generic slow gaze over a still and lonely looking landscape.

Characteristic of a film of a big foot sighting. It does not shed a good light on the reality of things.

We were one of three English households living among eleven Amish homes. From the time you turn onto our stretch of road you feel welcome. Mailboxes are adorned with flowers around their posts. Yards are clean, mowed and well-kept with decorative flowers and shrubbery.

With exception to the Bishops home. The rolls of fencing he ripped from the ground in front of our farm still sat untouched in his pasture along with bits and pieces of junk and old machinery for his cattle and horses to wander among.

Ill looking animals laid amongst the junk at times looking sad and hungry.

A run in shelter damaged by wind laid collapsed across the road from us as cows and horses stood around it in the hot sun, no trees in sight, wondering why they could no longer get inside for shade. Now and then a ping or bang was heard from an animal stepping on it.

Most others though, took pride in their homes and land. Strangers passing by would most likely see friendly waves from buggies and from small children playing in their family's yards.

Every now and then on face book someone would stand up for the Bishop. "Don't you think he's had enough?" "You've gone too far." Those comments made me feel heart ache to the core as I tried to shrug it off. They refused to read the book or learn about the situation.

What about us? We had more than enough. No one stood up for us. No one.

The Bishop and seller got everything they schemed, scammed and black mailed to get. The real estate company got their commission. The only thing we got, was taken advantage of. And for Gods sakes, my Mother was diagnosed and passed away in the middle of the whole thing.

Was there any compassion at all in those nay Sayers hearts?

They say the top three stresses in life are a close family member passing away, your last kid leaving the nest and buying a house. All three of those things happened in a single month. People asked me how we did it. There was no choice but to be strong. No choice.

Prayer is what held me together when I felt like falling apart. That's how I did it.

Dan and I were left with an unexpected financial disaster and someone else's mess to clean up. It would take years to get our train back on its tracks.

Isn't it us who they should say had enough?

It was time to remember that people are people. Without knowledge about the situation on their part, it would only be a frustrating, losing battle to debate.

I would let it rest in God's hands and keep my prayers focused that, no matter who they were or what they said, that they would never have to feel the desperation we felt the summer of 2012.

Now it was the first week in September 2013 and the summer was slipping away. Morgan announced she would be taking her horses to the new place she and her boyfriend would be renting. They were moving to the rented farm we came from.

I smiled inside knowing I'd still be traveling that road I grew up on. Driving past that house that built me, to visit her.

I would miss the presence of her horses here at the farm. Four would be with her, leaving us with our three. Tyke, Blessing and Rean. The pasture would feel almost empty.

Tyke was looking fly. He had gained weight and no longer showed a tailbone. I had started to feed him senior feed every night earlier in the summer and then the two of us would head to the lawn for a little spoiling.

There's just something about a warm summer night and a tall handsome old gelding on the end of a lead rope, eagerly grazing on new grass. My worries over if he would gain enough weight to get through the winter were fading.

Bad memories were being replaced with good and Dan and I soaked up every one of them. The Amish children especially always made us smile inside.

One day as we were traveling up our dirt road we saw two young Amish boys on a small wagon pulled by a mini pony. The pony was running mock ten and the boys were holding on tight while the small, close to the ground wagon seemed to be running out of control on its four wheels. Their smiles were beaming so bright they could have lit up the hill. We drove past them, smiling ourselves as we kept watching through the rear mirrors of the car.

Suddenly, the wagon was on two wheels and one of the boys was tossed off regardless of his efforts to hang on tight. We were going slow enough to see that they were okay and we continued on our way. Boys will be boys. Tough little buggers.

Not too long after that we went to the feed mill to get grain and dog food. I recognized the two boys from the wagon incident.

They stood still and quiet in front of a nearby pile of bags of grain. They looked sober and expressionless as I looked their way and I wondered if they had reached the age of learning English.

"Was that you boys who wrecked the wagon the other day?" Two small faces burst alive with smiles. "Yes!" "What's your horses' name?" I said. "Ranger" One of them replied.

A flood gate of chatter between Dan, the kids and myself emerged. They love their horse and it was clear to see the many times we had watched them, that Rangers love for them was returned.

In a sense, we all have our own "reality show." We can create our own over blown drama and keep ourselves and everyone around us in upheaval or we can chose to feel blessed for what we have and pay attention to what God wants us to do next.

A lot of those thoughts came when writing the books. We could hound the Amish, spice things up and create drama. We're not that kind of people. Never will be.

In many of these reality shows there is a tiny disclaimer like "This show has fictional characters for dramatic purposes."

That's not reality.

10
The Ride

I missed riding. I took Blessing out alone one day. A short ride up the road where everything was new to her. She hadn't been out of the pasture much and I was sure she would be slightly spooky at the new surroundings. I would be cautious and go slow and easy. I'd show her there was nothing to be scared of.

Not too far from home she started to get restless. She didn't want to move forward and started to prance. It wasn't Blessing at all, to get excited.

I sensed this wasn't from being barn sour. Something was wrong. In fear of a sudden uncontrollable bolt for home, I quickly dismounted but not so quick that I didn't see a flash of black in the pasture above us. A bear.

Standing on the ground, I held her reins tight as

she lifted her head in the air and let out warning snorts. Her head tossed. Her foot was pawing at the dirt. Her eyes wild. I slowly turned her in the direction of the farm and with a calm voice assured her we were okay, patting her neck from time to time. Letting her know everything would be alright as we walked back to the farm. That place that felt comfortable. That place that felt safe.

I knew we would have to take the same path again to get her over her fear. I did just that on a beautiful bright sunny day. I would kill two birds with one stone. I would take Bless for a quiet walk and take the camera along to capture those beautiful fall colors against that bright blue sky.

I would walk her to the top if the hill and take a panoramic picture of Gods amazing art work.

"Dan, I'm going to take Blessing for a walk, do you and Rox wanna go?

"Sure, why not." He said.

There we were, making our way up the road. With a camera in one of my hands, a horse on a lead rope in the other and a black lab dancing at our heels. We walked along and talked, taking in the sun and fiery colors of that fall day. Life didn't get better than that.

At about the same time, out from the corner of our eyes we saw a figure walking parallel to us in the pasture to our right. It was the bishop's pasture.

We knew right away who it was because of his lanky frame and the way he walked. It was the bishop. He was walking toward but beside and above us. What was he doing way out in the middle of his pasture? He was obviously walking home.

Dan and I kept our eyes and ears on each other, pretending not to see him. Pretending he was invisible. I felt the camera strap on my neck.

"Dan, take Blessing, I want to take a picture." "Want me to do it?" Dan said. "No, I got this. This will be great for face book"

Dan took the lead rope as I ducked behind Bless and snapped a shot. Got it.

A picture of the Bishop walking on the horizon with his back to us. It was a symbolic looking picture. He was walking away.

We continued on with our walk and didn't dwell on the past. We looked to the future. The world was at our feet. We reminded ourselves that everything was in God's hands. What was meant to be, would be. As we stood there at the top of the hill and looked down over at our farm below, we felt blessed. We saw the horses. The goats and that beautiful farm we called home.

I never did post that picture on face book.

Something inside said no. Don't lower yourself to that. I listened. It was one of those times when you don't want to listen to your gut but you know that you have to stay true to yourself.

Sometimes that's not the fun thing to do but in the end you know it's the right thing to do.

October was here and the leaves were turning beautiful shades of orange and yellow. Green and browns. Stunning. Dan and I had been working so hard cleaning up the farm all summer long. There hadn't been much time for fun. No time for riding.

I wondered if my horse would even remember the feel of a saddle during a lengthy ride. I missed it so much.

Before we bought the farm, Dan and I used to take long rides almost every night when he got home from work. Those rides were "our" time away from the world.

On warm days I wandered out to the middle of the pasture, clapping my hands together as I walked, alerting Tyke to my existence. Most days he'd lift his head and then go about his grazing. He knew when dinner time was. Clapping in mid- afternoon was a rouse to him and he knew it. He had gained a considerable amount of weight and was looking good. My old boy would make it through another winter.

I would make my way from horse to horse to say hello and the goats would follow hoping I would have a treat in my pocket. On one particular day one of the goats were missing. Pepper. Our big Boer goat wether. He had made his way through a hole in the gate and into the next pasture.

Not knowing how to get to me as I sat there in the grass with the two alpine kids we recently acquired, Pepper made his way to the road. I frantically ran to the fence to try to get to him. One speeding driver and Pepper would be hit. The Amish build good sheep fence. Nine strands.

I searched for a place to squeeze through as the Alpines followed behind. I pried open a spot and slipped out catching a piece of my jeans on the barbwire.

As I approached him, Pepper calmed down from his blatting fit and all was well. I knew he would stay beside me for the walk down the dirt road home.

It's not every day you see a woman walking the road with a giant goat at her heels. Even here in the middle of an Amish community.

As we were walking I saw an open buggy approaching. An older Amish couple, very sober looking. No eye contact. I wasn't sure they would even say hello. Regardless I smiled and said hi. As they rolled by the woman's eyes smiled at me. "Now that's a big goat!" She said as they traveled along.

Life was so special. Cherished. We had come so far.

One especially beautiful night I found Dan on the farm, busy cleaning. "Dan, stop what you're doing, we need to go for a ride" he agreed. I clapped for Tyke and he ran to me for his night time grain. Our mares followed close behind. An easy catch for us.

I led Blessing to the outside of the barn where her saddle and bridle were waiting. It had been too long since I had thrown that old Aussie saddle over her back and climbed up on her for a ride beside Dan and Raen.

I had missed that. I had missed her. Once an ugly duckling of sorts, Blessing had turned into a beautiful mare. She was no longer a solid brown color with the face of a mule. She was a beautiful appaloosa, her coat got lighter in the summers and her spots changed to a different pattern with every year that passed.

I had packed my camera in my saddle bag hoping to get some good shots of the landscape, so rich with color and then Dan and I headed off down the road.

Him on Raen and me on my Bless. We would ride to the main road and back. It was all new surroundings to the horses. I had hoped they would do well. There were cows. Dogs. Sheep. More horses than could be counted on each side of the road. How they would handle the ride was yet to be known.

As we made our way past the Bishops home we noticed it looked so secluded. So quiet. Bare. We thought the family must be away somewhere. No sign of life.

Further down the road calves in a field were playing. I felt Blessing tense up but a soothing voice and a calm pat to her neck told her they were okay and weren't out to get her. We rode to the end of the road without incidence but not without consequence. It felt like we were in a movie. In the twilight zone. A strange sense of quiet clung to the air around us.

Those Amish who weren't already outside enjoying the warm fall night, seemed to come outside as we made our way down the road. Just to look at who was on the horses. I think that's when it really hit us that we were the minority in the community. Although an awkward feeling at the time, we didn't mind. It's almost as if we were being shown what it's like to be different.

We had turned around and made our way almost home when we came across the Bishops son headed to the phone booth. His children were with him and one of his daughters made eye contact with me. An adorable child with her hair tucked into a head wrap that as unable to contain wisps of curly blonde locks. Her eyes were big and blue and full of wonder. As were mine.

What did she think of me, sitting high on top of a spotted horse, Levis and a flannel shirt, a baseball cap with a long curly blonde ponytail protruding out the back? I will always wonder what her eyes were asking or saying.

Aside from her dress and head covering, she was me, years and years ago. A simple life filled with family and church. Back yard games of hide and seek and kick the can. Pretending the cat, or in my case, one of the puppies my father raised to sell, was a baby doll. Chores to do and school to go to.

But as adults we would be so much different.

She would never know the freedom of independence. She would never know what it was like to spin tires or dance at a club or sit at a camp fire with friends until the wee hours of the morning.

Or to ride a horse in Levis, a flannel shirt, and a baseball cap with a long curly blonde ponytail protruding out the back.

And I would never know what it was like to be Amish. I would never understand why my God loves me for who he created me to be and is forgiving of my sins as I take this walk toward heaven that we're all taking, while their God is unforgiving and has the Amish religion and a Bishop as a middle man between him and them. There is no middle man between my God and me. It's just "us."

It's not for me to understand.

Life is a difficult thing. I feel its purpose is to help each other get through it. Black, white, Amish, English, straight, gay, rich, poor, we all have something in common. We all have souls. We all have inner struggles. We all hurt. Most importantly, we all need each other.

As far as heaven goes, I have no doubt I'll be there someday. I work at it every day by being a good person. I'm by far not perfect but I do ask for forgiveness when I need to and I give thanks every night for what I have.

I believe that heaven is a different place for everyone. My heaven will be seeing my Mom and Dad and Candy. It will hold a field of all the animals I've lost in my life. It will be warm and bright and peaceful. Wild flowers everywhere. That's what my heaven will be like.

11
Hey, Hey, Hey, Goodbye.

The first book had been an enormous success. The cash flow from it, not so much. We quickly discovered that for every one book sold about twenty people were borrowing it from someone to read. That was okay. I reminded myself that the story was the important thing. If we could help one family, that was what mattered the most.

We wanted our story told and were hoping that the book would be passed among our Amish community so they could see the truth. It was.

It was not only read by a few Amish families in our community but by other Amish in other communities as well.

Many comments were directed at how we were able to hold our tongues and not storm the Bishops house and just kick him in the shins or give him a piece of our minds the previous summer.

Money. Our future. It was all in his hands and he knew it. We could do nothing that might have risked losing the farm.

To raise a big stink after the sale with media and picketers and parties would have drawn attention to not just him but to the whole community. They did not deserve that. Their reputation was being hurt enough by their own Bishop.

It had been months and the seller never did get ahold of our lawyer to "make things right" as he said he would. Why did we even believe he would? Because he said he would. In our world a man's word is worth more than anything on paper. He was not a man.

I wrote our lawyer and sent the remaining balance of what we owed, along with a book. I requested that she send another letter with a concrete date for settlement. If things weren't settled by November 1st we planned to sue. We were done waiting.

We felt like fools for believing in his word.

Dan and I had been keeping busy working in the upper part of the barn. There was a room off the mow that needed attention. The floor was inches deep with chicken manure and chicken wire. Old boards and baling twine. Pieces of metal and broken plastic and glass protruding from the manure. Off from that room was a wall. Behind it a large metal grain bin still half full of grain, rotted and moldy, we decided that it was probably the reason rats were infesting the barn.

The rats were everywhere. They made their way into the horses' water buckets to drown and die. They were in the stall walls. Outside in the corn crib. A nest of baby rats was buried in a small Amish cart filled with rubbish. I found them as I was cleaning it out.

We hauled the junk out first, filling an entire trailer up with rubbish. Then we put on dust masks and got down to the business of clearing the floor of chicken manure. Even with the masks it became overwhelming and we'd have to step outside, only to get back at it moments later. Chiseling, shoveling, sweeping. It went on for hours. Our anger was our fuel. Dan removed the partition in the wall to expose the grain bin and released the bad grain down a chute to the lower part of the barn. The pile was enormous and full

99

of mold and rat droppings. The bad grain would be shoveled up into the tractors bucket and taken to a place the horses and goats couldn't get to. Eventually the grain bin was dragged outside to sit by the shop.

The mow had gained a big, open clean room. It would be our tack room.

One early fall evening we had a visitor. An Amish friend. We got to know him throughout the summer. Nice guy. Very horse oriented. A hard working man we both liked. I had been wanting to meet is wife but it just hadn't happened yet. It had been such a busy summer. I was sure we would meet soon.

"I was wondering, would you be interested in boarding a few horses up in your pasture for about a month? I'll pay you." He said.

In my head I was thinking sure, no problem. Those pastures had only been used for hay and we weren't going to use them. With all the pastured land we had, there was more than what we needed.

Our animals would continue to stay in the pasture by the house.

I looked at Dan to see if I could figure out his thoughts before he said anything. He gave me the same look. I opened up.

"I don't see why not but there is no gate on the upper pasture." With some discussion we all decided that he could bring his horses here for a month in exchange for a new gate for the pasture they would occupy. Done deal. Cool.

The conversation turned in a new and unexpected direction.

"I just came from signing a sales agreement with the bishop. I'm going to buy his farm. He's leaving. He's moving to Ohio."

Our faces stayed in a calm stance. Our souls did not. Inside my heart was singing "ding dong the witch is dead, the wicked witch, the wicked witch…." There were munchkin's dancing, rainbows forming, colored bubbles and horses of different colors prancing around everywhere. I was Glenda wearing that big pink bubblegum colored dress. Smiling. Waving a sparkly wand.

I (sort of) gained my composure and listened to what Dan was going to say, trying my hardest not to spontaneously burst out in applause.

"When are you moving in?" Dan said.

Our friend replied that if everything went well, it would be in the spring. I could not hold it in.

"We'll be SO happy to have you as a neighbor!" Our friend looked at me and smiled.

With a little more chit chat and discussion over the grain bin he was interested in and when the horses would be brought to the pasture, our friend was on his way home.

Dan and I looked at each other with the same look. I said "It didn't have to be this way. All he had to do was to return what he took, pay us for the mess we had to clean up and apologize to us and his community for what he did to them and to us and life could have gone on. Instead he's like a rat jumping off a sinking ship. He's just going to go to another community and be the same person he was here."

Just like the seller, he was a bad apple. Neither had any concern for anyone but themselves.

12
Echoing Laughter

Before our friends horses could be put in the upper pasture a gate had to be in place and water would have to be hauled and a tank filled. It was time. We saw the new red gate. We saw the wagons heading up the road.

"Dan, let's go up there and see if they need any help. I have been wanting to meet is wife anyway. Let's go!" We jumped into the truck and headed up the road to the pasture.

Dan helped to put the gate on, leaving at one time to grab a tool or two from the house. All in all there were three men. Dan and two Amish. I didn't see English or Amish. I only saw three men working together.

I wandered into the pasture to meet the young lady walking toward me. "Hi, I'm Lori, I been wanting to meet you so I told Dan we had to come up here!" I've been wanting to meet you too!" She said.

A beautiful girl with a wholesome look, she introduced herself.

Not far away was a toddler playing on a stone boat in the pasture. Smiling she pointed to the child and told me her name. The love in her eyes for that little girl was as bright as the fall leaves. With just a few German words, the little girl teetered towards her through the grass and was in her arms and on her hip.

The conversation between us flowed easily. I knew I had found a new friend.

Meanwhile, the gate had been installed and her husband had brought a wagon pulled by two powerful Belgians into the pasture.

It carried large barrels of water that would be dumped into a tank for the horses' water supply.

The two Amish men stood atop the wagon to tip and Dan stood on the ground below to guide and support the barrel. Suddenly there was a loud sound and followed by a splash. The barrel unexpectedly fell causing Dan to take the brunt of the barrel of water. Laughter echoed across the hill and into the warm night air.

We were all laughing. We were all smiling. We were all making memories. That's all we ever wanted.

A few days later the horses were brought to the pasture. Although they were quite a distance from the house, we were able to enjoy them from afar, against that beautiful skyline.

October was coming to an end and we didn't hear anything from our lawyer or from the seller. We would wait a couple more weeks and then mail him ourselves.

The weather was becoming a bit chilly and damp. On cold rainy nights I started to put our old boy in the barn to grain him with his senior feed and that's where he would stay for the night. Mornings I would walk to the barn and yell "Tyke!" He always answered me with a loud throaty hello whinny from behind the barn door. Always made me smile, to hear his hello.

It was always such a great beginning to my day. Routinely eager to get out of that stall and into the pasture, when I cut him loose from the halter and lead rope, off he would go out at a gallop calling to his mares.

One morning when Dan happened to be home with me, we noticed something odd. The pasture behind the farm housed Tyke, Blessing and Rean. The furthest pasture from the house was where our Amish friends' horses were being boarded. The middle pasture had no occupants. It had no gate and wasn't being used and yet, there were five big beautiful horses in it. Our reactions were, well that's odd. No worries on our part, they weren't harming a thing.

The pasture had been hayed and there was some good grazing in there. They were probably in heaven. We were sure their owner would come get them when he realized they were missing and sure enough, he did.

I was letting Deja outside and had her by the collar. Upon opening the door I was face to face with an Amish gentleman. "Hang on just a minute, let me put her back in her cage." I said. We had guests from Wyoming that weekend and Dan was inside cooking breakfast for them.

I opened the door to a cheery smile. "Hi Lori" I smiled back. "Hi, I'll bet you're looking for your horses." We both laughed as he introduced himself and explained he had been lying awake all night wondering where they went.

Silly thing for horses to get loose and let themselves into a pasture.

I had seen the Amish man around before but had yet to meet him. He stuck out to me because he always looked so happy. Some people just have that twinkle in their eye all the time. Another very personable and friendly Amish person. He said he would like to help with moving the store to the road. We chatted for a bit about his hand made leather items and the possibility of selling what he makes in my store when it's up and running.

We said or goodbyes and he was off to get his horses.

I sighed a deep breath. We were getting to know more and more of the Amish. Sharing laughter and smiles. We needed that.

Our pasture land

13
We'll Ride Again

My normal morning routine was to walk down to the barn with Roxy in tow. I'd head to the goat pen and let them out into the bigger pasture first, before letting Tyke out. This morning, however, I chose to do something different. Tyke was inside the barn because of a hard steady cold rain the previous night.

Being the end of October, it was time to start feeding him his grain twice a day. The new feeding schedule would begin that morning before I let him out to be with his mares.

I decided to get him started on eating his grain and go tend to the goats while he was feeding. I made a turn toward the barn. "Tyke!" I yelled as I approached the barn door. There was no loud whinny in return. I knew something was wrong. I pulled open the door. He wasn't looking over the stall toward me.

"Tyke?" I said hoping for an answer. Nothing. I slowly walked to the box stall he was in and peered in. He was laying on the floor of the stall. Upright, as if he was just tired out and resting.

"Tyke?" I said as I slid open the stall door. "Come on Tyke, get up. It's time to go out. It's time to see your girls."

I was hoping for a reaction. Hoping for him to wake up and turn toward me. Hoping he was just in a deep sleep. Hoping for any movement at all. Praying it was a bad dream.

Hope was quickly lost. Tyke was gone.

I slowly shut the stall door behind me and hung my head. There were no tears. There was only emotional numbness. I felt my own blank stare.

Walking out the barn door and into the driveway, I stood there quietly, hands in pockets and head still hung on that rainy October morning.

I heard myself start to say NO. Over and over, louder and louder as my feet moved me forward and I found myself starting to make my way to the house.

Once inside I broke down in tears and heard my own voice as I sobbed uncontrollably. "How could this happen? He was doing so well. He had enough weight to get through the winter and he seemed so happy and full of life. I don't understand. I just don't understand."

I didn't know how I would tell Morgan. She would be as shocked and as heartbroken as I. I needed to gain my composure to make that call to her. With a lump in my throat I called her.

"Morgan? Tykes Gone"

I could hear the tears in her voice as she replied "No. How? Why?" We spoke for a few minutes and she said soon she would be on her way.

I found myself needing to go back to the barn. I wanted to know what happened. I wanted to look for signs of what could have happened. I wanted to say goodbye to Tyke.

I opened the stall door and stepped in, crouching down at his rear. My hand slid through his thick soft coat over top of his magnificent blanket of spots just as I had done before as he laid in that same position warming himself in the summer sun. His long black and chestnut colored tail was laid out like a flag and I ran my hand through it catching my fingers in its thickness. I made my way to his head taking in the feel of his coat along the way and then I saw something I would never forget.

His neck was arched. His eyes were open. His ears were forward. He looked happy, like he could see where he was going and couldn't wait to get there. There were no signs of distress at all in his handsome face. Just a month prior I had taken a picture of him with that same look as he headed to his mares. A unique picture with prism's and sunlight rays around him. A heart shaped spot on his back side.

I stroked his neck and felt his ears from the base to the tips in wonderment. God had given me a gentle separation from my friend.

He was in his mid-thirties yet he would never have to suffer from the aging process that was sure to catch up with him. I would never have to make a heartbreaking decision to put him down. He was taken before those things happened.

Sometimes we don't understand the reasons that things happen. Often it takes years before we can look back and see the succession of life and how we got to where we are and why things had to happen the way they did.

It didn't take years or even months to understand why, when Tyke passed. It only took prayer and an open heart and mind, to understand what was meant to be.

I understood. I accepted. I felt grateful that my last memory of seeing him wasn't one I'll need to always try to shake. It's a memory I'll always embrace.

We'll ride again someday, Tyke.

Rest in Peace my Friend

14
Jar of Trinkets

The sign that once gave our road a name as you ventured off the main black top road was still gone. Never replaced from the time it was broken the previous spring. The road signs above the farm were now gone as well. All of them. A familiar yellow sign with an Amish horse and buggy symbol lay in a ditch at the bottom of the hill.

Our road was now marked with black and white Amish signs pointing the way up the hill and into the heart of Amish homes with businesses. The road stretched for three miles with our farm in the midst of the travel.

One Amish sign in particular stood out. The other Amish signs were clean and neat and welcoming. This sign was old and rusting and had broken off its bracket on one side. It still hung by what seemed like a thread. Dangling.

Symbolically swaying in the wind. Looking as if it could fall at any time. It was the bishop's business sign.

November 1st had passed. We assumed a follow up letter wasn't sent so we decided to take that on ourselves. We were hoping a deadline to settle would bring the response we were looking for. A check for settlement. It would end this and save us both from a court date.

The seller had a chance to redeem himself. If we heard no response back by December 1st, we would take that as a "go ahead and sue us."

All bets would be off as far as the settlement offer. The letter was mailed and we went on with life assuming that the seller wouldn't respond until the very tail end of November.

Some folks who read the first book were equally as upset at the real estate as they were at the Bishop. Us too. "They shouldn't get away with their actions without repercussions." They said. We were strongly urged by others to report them to the state of Pennsylvania. We did so in Mid-November. We filed a complaint and sent evidence of the deception during the sale. It was in the states hands rather or not they felt we had a case. Not long afterward we were sent case numbers. There would be an investigation.

The boarded horses had been in the upper pasture now for two or three weeks and they had it ate down quite well. Their owner stopped one day to ask about moving them to the middle pasture and maybe boarding them for a little bit longer. Instead of putting a gate where the gate was missing, he would use strands of wire or find another way to close up the pasture. Dan and I both agreed this would be fine and told him that there would be no charge for using the middle pasture or for keeping the horses there longer than was originally planned.

They weren't hurting a thing and we were loving how they added life to those empty fields.

His wife, my new Amish friend came inside one night with a garbage bag in tow while her husband talked to Dan outside about buying the grain bin we had taken out from the barn.

She opened the bag to expose a big glass jar with a teddy bear and some blocks painted on it. The blocks were stacked and spelled "baby." The top of the jar was painted pink and its' inside was full of trinkets. Beads, pacifiers, blocks, small toys. She explained that many of the Amish have jars for their child's keep sakes.

She was requesting I do one for her little girl and had brought the jar as an example. I told her rather than keep it with me, I would take a picture and use the picture as a reference. She handed me a slip of paper with the information she wanted it to say.

I thought of something.

"Hey, do you sew? I have this quilt that my parents gave me a long time ago and stupid me put it in the washer and it ruined it. Some of the seams ripped. I'll trade you for painting the jar if you'll fix my quilt. I'm no good at sewing at all." I said.

She looked at me and smiled. "Well, I don't sew too much but I do make our clothes. I could look at it and see."

"That would be great. I'll have to get it out of the attic and get it to you sometime. It's really no hurry." I said.

I put on my boots and walked with her to the men, who were standing by the buggy chatting.

Her husband had the baby in his arms and looked like a natural at Fatherhood. He loved his family. It wasn't hard to tell. He could have made her take the baby inside with her while she talked with me about the work she wanted done. Instead, he tended to the little girl while his wife was inside with me. A man like that gets my attention. My respect.

We couldn't have been happier in knowing those two would soon be living next door.

With the end of November nearing, we hadn't heard anything in response to our letter to the seller about settlement. Right up until the last hour. Just as we had expected.

We were out shopping and when we arrived home we checked the mail. There was a slip of paper from the post office stating we had a registered letter we would have to sign for. It was from the seller.

We pondered all night about it.

"I'll bet he has realized that we aren't going to let this go and he is going to make things right."
"I'll bet that letter was sent registered because there is a check inside and this whole thing will

be over." "If there isn't a check in it why would he send it registered mail?" Questions ran between us over and over.

With memories of our conversations with him here at the farm still ringing in our heads about making things right with us, we were hopeful he was ready to prove he was a man of his word. We convinced ourselves that he would do the right thing. We would use some of it to buy new fencing panels. We would rent a backhoe to dig trenches in the barn. We would put some on the principal of the loan to put us back to where we should have been in the first place. Everything would feel right again.

I was at the post office as soon as it opened to collect our letter. I eagerly took it to the car and opened it. There was no check. Only a single piece of notebook paper. My heart dropped.

Hello,

This is in regard to your letter. We do not feel that we owe $10,000 we don't have that kind of money in the first place. We still have the paper on the agreement on the corral and the shelves. The stoves were removed before the contract was signed and besides the contract was expired.

The Bishop tried to contact you about cleaning out the barn and you did not respond. So there leaves little room to doubt that we could win in court. We made a 900 mile trip to try to settle this and you didn't want to. We have discussed this and decide to offer you $1,000. For cleaning the barn and saw mill. If you agree to this we will need to have something in writing and you will have the money by January 1st 2014.

I will be keeping a copy of this for our records.

Signed by the Seller and his Wife

A lump formed in my throat. Both sadness and anger overcame me at the same time. How could anyone be so devastatingly dishonest and so harshly uncaring? My mind was drawing a blank as to why or how he thought he could get away with any of this.

Contract or not contract, what made him think any of this was right? What made him think we should be held accountable and responsible for cleaning up after him? What made him think he could accept an offer and then take things?

When Dan read the letter he was angry. "Call the court and get things going. He gave me his word. I've had it. I've just had it!"

I replied "Dan, we need to wait. We need to take them and the real estate to court at the same time. We have done nothing wrong here. We need to see them both in court so that we can watch them explain to a judge and maybe even a jury why they put us through so much hell. I want to hear their explanation's in front of others. We have a case opened with the state of Pennsylvania as far as the real estate goes. It could help us in court. Let's see what happens with that first."

15
An Amish Christmas

December was here and the winter had seemed easier than the previous year. Still had snow. Still had cold but we were down to two horses and three goats. Dan had rented a back hoe to dig holes for posts for the run in shelter and the posts where set. We had ordered wood from a local Amish man to build the run in but since the wood was drug out of the forest by horses we had to wait until the ground froze. That was okay.

The two stalls we had would house our mares and the goats would be comfortable in their pen attached to a big wooden box for shelter.

I wouldn't mind the work of putting them all in every night when it was cold or stormy and putting them all back out come mornings. Didn't really like the constant stall cleaning but it was good exercise and I rested better at night knowing they were tucked in. Safe and warm.

They deserved it after the harsh winter the previous year.

Orders for my art work were coming in heavy. I lived and breathed for my work in December. One customer was my Amish friend from up the hill who brought me a beautiful hand crafted wooden framed mirror she had bought her husband. She wanted his name and a standard breed horse painted on it.

Dan's black lab, Roxy slept at night in her beloved cage. Every now and then when Dan was rushing around for work he'd forget to lock her back in her cage after he let her out to pee. She'd lay there hoping he didn't notice and as soon as she heard that truck start and pull away, there she'd go. Through the kitchen, across the living room, up the stairs, down the hall and onto the bed with me. I always woke up when Dan got up from bed to go to work. I always knew when a big black lab had outsmarted her master. I could hear her coming.

After a little discussion with Dan about how she would be no good in protecting me if she was locked in her cage while he was gone, it was her ritual every morning to get in bed with me when he left for work. The new routine was Dan getting up and ready for work and when it was time to go out the door he'd say "Go get momma." Off she would go like a thoroughbred from a starting stall. With one large morning leap she'd be in bed with me, always making sure I was there by lifting the covers from my face or head before settling down beside me to sleep until it was time for me to get up. From then on I slept like a baby at night.

In mid-December I received a call. It was from an investigator from the state of Pennsylvania. He was assigned to investigate our complaint against the realty. He needed to talk to Dan and I. Dan was still working seven days a week and couldn't take off from work so the investigator came to the house to meet with me and we went over everything together.

Information was requested and I promised I would get it to him ASAP. Between the investigation and my orders, my mind was whirling and sleep was rare.

Christmas was nearing. Although I had tried my hardest there wasn't much time to take a step back and enjoy the holiday season. I grasp at every moment I could to celebrate the birth of Jesus. Five plates of cookies and candy were hand delivered or set at our door from Amish neighbors. Their Christmas spirit gave me sighs of happiness.

I had been saving my Amish friends work till last. I had to get Internet orders and other local orders out the door first.

Christmas Eve was a blustery cold day with snow and wind. She arrived that morning in her horse and buggy to collect her art work. Her husband was away hunting so she was sneaking down to pick it up before he returned home. "I'm so sorry." I said. "It's not done yet but I'm close! Can you come back later?"

As bubbly as ever she said that was no problem, she could come back.

As the day progressed there as more snow. More wind. By late afternoon the work I did for her was done and I hated the thought of her having to harness up her horse again for the trip down the hill in all that wind and cold when I had a car I could drive. Dan was gone with his truck Christmas shopping.

My car sat outside in the blowing snow and wind as I agonized about driving it up the hill.

Would I make it without going in a ditch? Would their drive way be plowed?

I had a fear of driving in the snow. I've had that fear for a very long while and it was crippling at times. In 2008 I was one of eight women picked to do a "Clean Start Challenge" for the Lifetime TV's web site. They picked eight women from thousands who wanted to change their life in one way or another. I wanted to conquer my fears. I had so many. Winter driving was one of them. Getting behind the wheel meant panic. A racing heart. A lump in my throat and sometimes, even tears.

We were given web cams and had to do weekly updates on our progress. I was so crippled by winter driving that at times I didn't even take my daughter to her bus stop for fear of the drive.

By the end of the "Challenge" I was driving her to the bus stop every morning. I was driving to my parents' house in snow storms. I was driving everywhere. Back then, I had something to prove to all those people watching my videos.

I had put myself out there. I couldn't hide anymore. I had to prove I was strong and that I could change not only for myself but for my daughter who needed a strong confident role model.

That was years ago and as the wind blew and the snow piled up I felt that old panic looming in the back of my mind trying to push aside my confidence. Trying to cripple me again.

I had my coat and boots on and off several times before I got up the courage to chance it. To talk myself into it. And then, off I went out into the snow, headed to the car.

As I was backing out of the drive I saw an Amish boy walking toward me. It was too cold and wintry to be out walking. Did he want something or was he on his way somewhere up the hill?

I started to drive away slowly and his pace picked up. He had something in his hand. Was it for me? I rolled down the window and waited for him to arrive at the car.

"These are for you and Dan" he said, handing me a plate of cookies and candy. "How nice, thanks so much." I replied. Smiling, we both said Merry Christmas and he made his way back down the hill.

I rolled the window back up and took a deep breath. Driving slowly with both hands on the wheel, I made it up the hill and pulled into the drive way as the snow and wind whirled around my car.

I flung open the car door hanging on tightly to the box that held the painted mirror. It was closed and taped just in case her husband was home. Couldn't ruin the surprise!

She opened the door and was seemingly surprised to see me. "You brought it up?"

"Yes" I said as I opened the box for her to inspect my artwork. She was pleased. Looking at me with a smile she asked "How much do I owe you?"

"You don't owe me anything. Sometimes I like to simply pass along the gift that God gave to me. If I can do without the money, the happiness of giving my blessing away is worth more than that. Merry Christmas."

She smiled. "Thank you! Merry Christmas to you too!" We said our goodbyes and I headed back to the car feeling good inside. My last piece of artwork that was ordered, was delivered. I was finally done after hours and hours of all-nighters' constantly battling a mental fog of preoccupation with my work.

Suddenly I was able to slow down. It was Christmas Eve. There was still time to enjoy the holiday.

Smiling and suddenly feeling a combined burst of confidence and Christmas spirit, I drove fearlessly back down the hill to the farm, taking the plate of cookies I was given, into the house with me to add it to the others on the table. I sighed a happy sigh.

That Christmas was like no other. It was while sitting quietly and watching our children, that I understood the sense of pride and happiness that was felt by my parents to have their family all together in the same place. Laughing. Talking. Smiling. Bonding.

16
Black Ice

The winter had been so long. The most brutally cold winter I had ever remembered in my lifetime. As much as I loved our animals and loved taking care of them, the trips to the barn each morning and night became dreaded. With no run in shelter for them yet, they were put in at night and put back out mornings. I promised them this winter would be better. I would keep that promise.

Some mornings the wind chill was thirty to fifty degrees below zero and although we kept the animals inside they still had to be fed and watered. During morning chores there was numbness in my fingers and toes no matter how many layers of gloves and socks I put on. Every morning the water buckets would be frozen solid with any water the animals didn't drink while they had the chance. I had to bang and kick at the buckets to get the ice out of them so they could be refilled, only to be frozen again within hours. I used caution with each trip. If I were to fall or have an accident of some sort it would be a long while before Dan would be home. The winter was getting to us. All of us. Amish buggies braving the cold were far and few.

I used to keep the phone receiver upstairs in our bedroom but I had moved it so that late calls wouldn't disturb Dan and early morning calls wouldn't disturb me. My M. O. was to come down the stairs mornings, look at the answering machine and if it was blinking, tap the message button as I walked by it on the way to the coffee pot.

I did just that on Feb 2nd 2014.

"Lori, I've been in an accident. I totaled the truck." Still half asleep, not yet to the coffee maker, I stopped in my tracks to listen. "I'm okay, don't come out on these roads, they are bad." My heart raced as I quickly made my way to the art room to grab my phone. As I reached for it, it rang. My heart slowed down a beat when I saw the caller ID. It was Dan calling from work. "Are you okay?! What happened?!" I said. On the other end of the phone Dan assured me he was okay but his truck was not. "It's totaled. It's really bad. I was on my way to work and I hit a patch of black ice. I was doing about 55. I lost control and went off the road and hit some trees. There's not much left of the truck."

He went on to tell me that Matt, a fellow coworker and friend came upon the accident scene and stopped. He was in disbelief that Dan had survived. Matt stayed with him that morning until everything was taken care of. We are so fortunate that we know so many good, kind and caring people.

That evening I drove Dan to the accident scene so he could show me what happened. I didn't want to think about how horrific and sudden the accident must have been but the story was told plain as day with the skid marks and the damaged trees. One tree sure to be marred forever. A reminder of a miracle.

A short distance away was a lot where Dan's truck sat parked.

I pulled into the drive way. That beautiful truck was gone. Just gone. Almost unrecognizable. Every piece, every part had a dent or ding. The driver's side was crushed inward from the hit it took from the tree.

The box was hanging loose and the drive shaft was on the ground beneath it. All had been totally destroyed. Well, almost all.

The inside of the cab of the truck was intact. It had protected him. When the truck settled to a stop after such a wild whirlwind decent from the road, the driver's side door opened by itself. Dan stepped out and walked away.

In a daze he looked back at the truck to see if he was still inside it. Like in the movies, when you see yourself after you have passed on.

There were so many "ifs." The previous year during the winter Dan drove my S-10 to work to save gas.

"If" he had fixed it instead of me selling it, he certainly would have been driving it that day. There would have been no chance for survival in hitting black ice at 55 mph with my tiny truck.

Just a few days prior to his accident, his truck hadn't been starting because of the bitter cold weather and the diesel was gelling up, so he needed to use my car to get to work. The day of the accident, however, it did start and he was able to drive it.

"If" he had been driving my car the outcome may have been the same as if he had been in the S-10.

"If" he hadn't been wearing a seat belt. "If's" are so much easier to let go of when they aren't regrets. That's when "ifs" become blessings.

Dan's Mother passed away in a car accident when he was just a year and a half old. There had been several times in his life when he has felt she was watching over him. This was one of those times.

For the time being, Dan would have to drive my car back and forth to work until an insurance check arrived. I work at home and I could sacrifice my vehicle for a while. I'd have no way off the farm to run errands during banking and post office hours but we'd figure it out. I was just happy Dan was still here in my life.

Within two weeks an insurance check arrived. The loan on Dan's wrecked truck was paid off and we had nine thousand dollars to buy a new one. We felt it was a blessing in disguise. No more big truck payment. It was gone. We could get him a nice used truck for nine thousand and have no payment at all. We thought we might even get financially back on track quicker than was anticipated, from the farm buying fiasco that set us back so far. I could have the use of my vehicle again. Finally, the stress would be lightened. Dan had a truck all picked out.

My Twin Brother Larry agreed to drive us to where the truck was. We arrived in Titusville, PA around noon. There she was. Dan's dream truck. A white Ford F350 diesel duly. A private seller from Craig's list. The truck Dan had been talking about for the past week. I wasn't impressed. The windshield had two long horizontal cracks in it and when he started it the engine it choked and sputtered. I looked at the tires. Not much tread. The engine wasn't the original engine and the odometer was stuck on 100,000 miles. The owners guess was that it had about 145,000 on it.

My gut feeling said "are you crazy?" Off Dan went for the test drive. There was nothing I could say or do, I already knew that.

Dan and I are two different animals when it comes to two things. Trusting people and spending money. My lesson in life came in 1999 when I lost my cherished and hard worked for credit score and pretty much everything I owned too, because I fell in love with and married a con artist. Since that time, I investigate. I record. I think and I use my gut. That's why I had so much evidence on the Bishop, seller and real estate.

I would never allow anyone to take advantage of and run over me like that again. Ever. I had enough.

Because we're married, the money part of us may seem odd to some but it's what works for us.

Dan has his and I have mine. He pays his share and I pay mine. If I'm short and need help, he helps me and if he's short and needs help, I help him.

Somehow, we make it work.

"Did you know about that windshield?" I said to Dan when he returned from the test drive. "No, I'm going to try to talk him down. Follow us to the notary." Larry and I followed behind and noticed that one of the back tires was wobbling badly. Enough to worry my twin for our ride home. Dan assured us we would be okay for the three hour trip back home. Originally

Larry was going to cut off from us at a certain point but he stayed behind us for a long while, pulling off on a ramp to let us know that if anything happened to call him and he would come back. On the way home we discovered the passenger side window didn't work and the truck's doors wouldn't lock. I got an even deeper sinking feeling but remained quiet.

The next morning at sun rise I woke up and looked out the window. That truck was gone and my car was there. A peaceful feeling fell over me. It had been two weeks. I missed her. No more mileage on my car. No more wear and tear. She would be there for me to clean once a week and get into and go when I felt the winter blahs. My ticket to sanity was back. I took a shower and did my hair, ready to face the day. Ready to get in and go!

Smiling as I trudged through the snow, I got in and turned the key to warm her up. Sweet sound.

A few minutes later I went back to get in and drive away. As I pulled out in reverse I slid sideways. Forward again. Sideways again. You've got to be kidding. I said to myself out loud "Oh hell no!" and before I knew it, I was out of my parking spot and driving down the road. Sweet freedom. Sweet independence. It was back. I was back.

The next morning came too soon. 4:30 AM.

"Lori, my truck won't start. I need to use your car." My heart dropped. A storm was brewing both outside across the county and in my soul too. I would need to have strength to keep it together.

I needed to find peace inside for however many more weeks I would be stranded alone with no escape from these long winter days.

The deeper issue inside me was the miles accumulating on my car. I was so anal about that car.

I went out of my way to not put any unnecessary miles on it, even protesting six mile drives to one store as opposed to a sixteen mile trip to another store Dan was fonder of.

I averaged driving six miles a day and now my car was nearing three straight weeks of forty plus mile trips every day and coal for our stove was being loaded into the back of it whenever we ran out and needed a new supply. The heat pan to the muffler partially came off. The wiper blades where deteriorating and it was 1,000 over from needing an oil change. My heart was aching. There was a reason I was so emotionally attached to this car.

I spent most of my life as a single Mom. My kids' wants and needs always coming first, I had never been able to afford a nice vehicle. My Mom wanted me to have hers. She didn't want to leave this earth worrying about her baby in that beat up old S-10. She wanted that car to "putt, putt, and putt up that road to the farm."

In her car I felt she was still looking out or me. Still there.

The box of Kleenex in the back seat were there when I missed her and couldn't hold back the tears. She put them there herself shortly before she was diagnosed.

The gloves in the glove box kept my hands warm one day in below freezing temperatures as I pumped gas.

The bright pink umbrella that was under the seat was opened up and used on several rainy windy days.

Her car was my cherished connection and in a way it felt so "gone" from my life.

The winter had been too long. Normally I could pray and bounce back to a positive mode in no time but many days I caught myself spending hours just sitting. Sighing. Agonizing. Staring at nothing. The cabin fever felt intense at times. I was here 24/7 and just thinking about not being able to go anywhere even if I wanted to until Dan came home from work at night, started to feel so constrictively devastating.

I missed my Mom. There was no one to go to to make everything feel all better any more.

In my self-pity and depression I realized, yes, there was. There was someone who always made things feel all better.

My twin Brother, Larry.

Realizing this was worth the price of how the realization came to be. We had always been close but since Mom and Dad passed away that bond had grown even deeper between us.

I would pick myself up and dust myself off. I would be patient and put Dan's truck repairs in God's hands knowing sooner or later I would have use of my car again. I would use this as a learning experience. I would make a plan.

My plan was to save as much money as I could to buy a new little used truck in the fall. It wouldn't be easy but it would be a goal to meet and with a lot of hard work and doing without other things, I knew I could do it. I'd keep my car registered and insured but parked and would only use it on special occasions. I'd put my miles on my truck. That way, when Dan broke down I'd have an extra for him to borrow and still have a way off the hill for myself. Just like when I had my S-10. Perfect.

It's so easy to sit and feel self-pity but it's draining. Agonizing. Sometimes you just need to set a goal and make a plan to get excited about, to pull yourself out of the gloom and doom.

Dan worked hard and put so much time and money into the truck he bought until one day he was able to drive it to work. He was ecstatic! On his way back from work the tire that had wobbled during the test drive, blew. He limped the truck home and after shutting it off it wouldn't start again, no matter what he did. It was dead. He furiously called the guy he bought it from.

"This is Dan, the guy you sold the bleep piece of bleep truck to. You need to call me back." Of course there was no return call. He had $9,000 in his pocket, a piece of paper that said "as is" and no conscience in sight. There was no return call.

We had to regroup. We had to think about what to do. Continue to put money into that truck? Send it to a diesel mechanic? His last truck went to a diesel mechanic and didn't come back for almost two months. If we did that we'd have to buy something for Dan to drive back and forth to work. I wasn't willing to sacrifice my freedom to come and go for any longer than I had to. Three weeks had been long enough already. But what sense would that make? Buy a vehicle and pay a couple grand for repairs on the truck?

Dan was frustrated. I was frustrated. We decided our best bet was to call the lemon a wash. We would try to sell it with a list of all the problems and hope to get at least half of what we lost. Dan would find a used vehicle from a reputable dealer. He'd have to get a loan and he'd be back in the same position as he was before the accident.

We found a truck in Springville NY at a dealer. Just what Dan wanted and in the right price range. We made arrangements to go look at it and once again, Larry agree to drive us.

I was hurrying along with barn chores as Larry sat waiting in his truck. He had arrived to pick me up first and we would get Dan from work and be on our way for the hour and a half trip. As I feeding the goats I heard my name. "Hey Lor? Dan just called me. It's off for today, the dealer can't get the truck started."

Since Dan had already planned to take a half day off work we headed out anyway, for a truck shopping adventure. As tempting as buying a brand new truck would be and as quick a fix as it would be, that night we discussed how it might be a bad move.

It takes two of us to make it work here at the farm. If I were to get hurt or if he were to lose his overtime, a big and prolonged payment would hurt us immensely. We decided against it.

A couple days later on a Thursday the dealer from Springville called Dan once again. The truck had been fixed. It was ready for Dan to look at and take a test drive. He got a check from the bank for the purchase price just in case the truck was what he wanted. He got together all the information he would need, took another half day off work and he and Larry headed to Springville.

I heard from them later that day when the phone rang here at home. "Lori, we got here and they had the truck up on the lift in the shop because they couldn't get it started again before we got here. They're working on it. We're going to wait a little bit."

An hour passed and another call came with a very frustrated Dan, on the phone. "We're still waiting. This is bullshit. Why did they even call me to come? We are ready to just leave. I'm ready to just go buy that brand new truck and be done with it." I could feel his stress and told him my opinion. I asked for Larry's opinion. At the end of our call I said this to him.

"I will support you 100% in whatever decision you make. All I ask is that you don't make any decisions based on frustration. Above all, listen to your gut. We'll get through this. We'll figure it out"

Between calls from Dan I headed to the barn to let the animals outside. Normally I tried to clean the stalls every morning to save time on night chores. The manure was thrown into a pile on the concrete in the middle isle of the barn until Dan could take it out with the tractor.

The tractor had a flat. The tractor battery was needed in Dan's truck to help him get it going. In the meantime, the manure pile had grown quite large.

That morning as I let the horses out, I noticed smoke rising from the middle of the pile. Just a little but enough to concern me.

I told Dan about it on his next call. "It's not that bad right now, I'll keep my eye on it every hour. Don't worry over it, I got this." I said.

I put my boots and coat back on and went to check on the pile. More smoke. Or was it steam? I pushed a layer of manure back with a shovel and took my glove off. Heat. I decided I couldn't chance anything and would have to do the best I could to get it outside by hand. Dan was almost two hours away. This couldn't wait.

I slid the heavy barn door wide open and grabbed a pitch fork. I made trip after trip with the pitch fork. From the pile to the driveway. Spreading the smoking manure out in a single layer on the ground. Starting at the top of the pile

I went down through its core until I could no longer see any ash or smoke.

Mission accomplished. The day could move on.

It was almost dark when Larry and Dan arrived back home. That evening Dan said "Maybe there is a reason for what happened with that truck in Springville." I smiled widely. "I was thinking that same thing today. Maybe it was meant for you to figure out how to get that lemon running. Maybe you just needed a little break from it."

I had to figure out how to have patience, be supportive of Dan and deal with what was happening inside of me. I'm the kind to say "that's okay" when it's really not.

I suck everything up and internalize it, never wanting to say anything that might hurt anyone, including Dan.

This time it was hard to keep all those agonizing thoughts in. I was feeling trapped with no way to go anywhere and what my car was being put through with miles and wear and tear every day was killing me. If I mentioned it to Dan he became angry. He needed my support. I needed my sanity. There was only one thing to do.

There were a few coworkers in the area that Dan could ride in to work with. I suggested he use those rides so it wouldn't be so hard for me to figure out how to do the things I needed to do without the use of my car. He was reluctant. Some of it was that they went in an hour later than he. Most of it was that pride thing.

I turned the trip on in my car so I could no longer see the odometer. Silly, huh? But seeing it made me almost cry. To make myself feel even better I called a dealership and made an appointment for an oil change and tune up.

After all those rough country road miles put on her in such a short amount of time, things weren't sounding like they used to. She was aging much faster than I planned. So was I.

Making sure it was well taken care of would help me to get through the emotional attachment I had for it. It would give me peace of mind until we figured out what we would do.

The winter was wearing on us. Both of us. By mid-March Dan was still unable to get his truck running and by this time I was going on six weeks of not having a vehicle.

Most of Dans time was spent in the garage and he looked like he had aged ten years. Most nights I did chores alone. The water in the barn froze and I had to start carrying buckets of water from the house.

The manure in the barn was piling up in the isle way again from cleaning the stalls and the tractor still sat outside with a flat tire. Still missing it's battery.

Although there was no longer a truck payment for Dan to make, the money spent on fixing his new-to-him truck was taking a tole on his paycheck.

The work in the basement Dan started shortly before the accident stopped. The work on the run-in stopped. There would be no new dinning room that year.

It angered Dan if I complained about not having the use of my car. Being unable to go anywhere angered me. The winter was getting longer and longer. The tension between us grew more every day.

Sometimes life just throws you a curve ball and you have to do your best to hit it.

The hardest part is deciding the best way to hit it when it's coming at you.

Dans Wreck 2/2/2014

17
Life's Dances

"We have an appointment today" Dan said when he called from work. I couldn't think of what we would have an appointment for. "An appointment for what?"

He explained that there was a dodge truck for sale in my price range a short distance from his work. "Okay" I said.

I had just paid two credit cards off with my share of the taxes and for the first time in years I was able to financially breathe again. I barely had started to save for the truck I planned to buy with cash in the fall but I was alright with buying one with a loan if it could get us back to being "us" again. I missed us. I wanted things to go back to the way they were. I didn't care if it put me back in struggle mode.

This was the direction I had to hit that ball.

We pulled into the dealership. There it was. A 1998 dodge Ram 1500. Short box. Single cab. Slightly lifted. Mean looking tires. Mean looking truck. Burgundy in color, it had a black splotch on both sides where someone tried to do some art work that didn't turn out so well.

I didn't care. THIS was the truck. My truck.

Dan went over it with a fine tooth comb. Under it. Inside it. Behind it. We took it for a test drive and were both impressed. Once behind the wheel, pulling out into the road I squealed woohoo as I pressed the gas and realized its power.

Yes, I am a truck girl and I wanted this one. I trusted Dan in knowing what it was worth. What might need fixed. If he would have said he had major concerns I would have taken his word and walked.

He liked the truck too and before we knew it we were sitting inside the dealer's office negotiating a price.

Dan was cool and calm and smart. He wouldn't back down from his offer and nor would the dealer.

I decided to go get a coffee, a short distance away. When I returned the dealer was outside on his phone. I slipped in the door and took my seat beside Dan.

Not long after, the dealer came in with a piece of paper and set it on his desk in front of us. In big blue letters written in magic marker it said

"YOU WIN!!"

Dan got him down in price and got a thirty day or thousand mile warranty to boot.

The next day I got prepared for a three year loan. First vehicle loan I had since 1996.

I pulled out all of what I had saved, to pay for the taxes, registration and fees. I even had a little cash left to put toward it to save me from having to get a loan for the full purchase price.

I made a promise to myself that I would have it paid for within two years.

All was well with the world when I drove that truck home. It was my freedom. It was a way to get us back on the road we were on before the accident.

I didn't care how many miles got put on it. I didn't care if it got dirty. I didn't care if coal or saddles or motor parts were put in the back of it.

Dan could drive it to work until he got his truck figured out and I wouldn't have a second thought. There would be no more tension over my loss of a vehicle.

When he was done using my truck it would come in handy for me. I could use it for short errands to save mileage on my car. I could use it for farm work when Dan wasn't here and I needed to do some yard cleaning. I could use it for trips to the feed mill and tractor supply.

My troubles and worries seemed to wash away.

My car would be right there for me. Sitting in the driveway day after day. It would be home when I was home. Life felt good again. It could move on. Speaking of moving.

Every now and then when I got a free minute before bed I goggle the bishop and sellers name to see what I could find.

One night I found something that caused a little spark inside me.

154

The Bishop was having a moving sale.

APRIL 12, 2014

30 HOLSTEIN HEIFERS – HORSE – LIVESTOCK FARM MACHINERY – BUGGIES – PRODUCE EQUIPMENT FARM RELATED - HOUSEHOLDS AND MORE!

LIVESTOCK:

30 Yearling Holstein Heifers; Jersey Bull; 6 yr. old Standard bred Driving Mare; 35 Laying Hens, Turkeys, Geese, Pheasants.

FARM MACHINERY:

Waukesha Engine w/Clutch; IHC Green Crop Hay Loader; Hay Rake; Buck Rake; JD 14T Baler; Field Drags; 12' Harrow; Field Packer/Roller; 2 Hay Loaders needs repair; IHC Power Corn Sheller; 2 Row Corn Planter; JD Corn Binder w/Truck; McDeering 7' Grain Binder w/Truck; Field Sprayer; Lime Drill; 5 – 2 Way Plows; Oliver Plow; Fore Cart; Dump Trailer; Gravity Wagon; Flatbed Wagon; 50 'Hay & Grain Elevator; Round Bale Carrier;

Round Bale Feeder; 4 Feed Troughs; 2 Buzz Saws.

PRODUCE EQUIPMENT:

8' x 14' Fiberglass Greenhouse; Water Wheel Trans planter; Plastic Mulch Layer; Misc. Produce Supplies.

BUGGIES:

2 Seated Top Buggy; Single Seat Top Buggy; Open Buggy; 2 Bobsleds.

HAY:

Approx. 200 Bales of 2nd Cutting Hay

FARM RELATED:

Milking Stands for Goats; Lot of Cement Blocks; 3 Fuel Tanks; 14' Boat on Trailer; Horse Drawn Lawn Mower; Weed Eater; Misc. Farm Related Tools.

HOUSEHOLDS:

Enterprise Kitchen Range; Dressers; Tables; Folding Tables; Oak Sewing Machine Cabinet and Heads; Solid Oak Chairs; Knee Hole Desk;

Oak Wood Box; Oak Office Chairs; Office Desks; Beds & Cribs;; Rug Loom; Upright Ice Box; Maytag Wringer Washer; Rinse Tubs; **Shelving**; Table Top Cream Separator; Butter Churn; Butter Bowl; Crocks; Sad Irons; Misc. Dishes and Glassware; Box lots of Misc. Households.

NOTE:

Owners moving out of state. 9:30 AM Wagon Loads of Smalls, Households, Farm Machinery, Followed by Livestock

TERMS: Cash or Check w/Proper ID.

Lunch & Bake Sale by Amish Ladies
Restrooms

Shelving. He was selling our shelving. My thoughts were that he was probably selling our fencing too. It was still there. Still sitting in the same spot in his pasture as it was in July 2012. Close to the road so we could see it every day. It was put there when he ripped it out of the ground from in front of our house.

Who sells all of their things when they move? Beds? Dressers? Dishes? Everything? Don't they need those things at their new place? I didn't understand it.

I made a copy of the auction and circled the word "shelving" laying it on the table for Dan to see when he got up.

His simple answer to it when he called from work. "More salt in the wound." Was it really that much of a surprise?

The fencing panels where still at the bad seeds home. Right out there were we could see them, he rarely ever used them. They laid stacked up and leaned against another fence.

We saw the "bad seed" almost every day. The bishop's side kick in the theft of property. He always waved. Of course he waved. He didn't lose anything. He kept what he took from us.

Personally as much as I'd like to kill him with kindness and wave back I couldn't do it. To lift my arm and wave my hand would take effort and he wasn't worth that. Instead when Dan and I drove by we'd look straight ahead and do nothing. Unless of course his wife or kids were outside. They had done nothing and we would wave at them.

There is just so much we didn't understand about the Amish culture and how the bad seeds in such a religious sect are allowed to exist without repercussion.

My God gave me a conscience to know right from wrong. My God would never let my heart get away with the things the bishop did to us or to his community.

We all have a voice inside of us. We call it our gut instinct. If we go with our gut we make the right choices.

Until I was in my late thirties I didn't listen to my gut. I listened to what and who everyone wanted me to be and not to that voice in my head leading me to where I should have gone. I wanted to make everyone around me happy and I was forgetting one person in that equation. Me. Sometimes when people think they know what's best for you it isn't really you they are thinking about. It's really what's best for them.

There came a point in my life when I had lost almost everything. I got through it in time and got into another bad relationship and ended up losing everything I had that I had left to lose. My car. My furniture. My friends. Rock bottom. I was stuck in a bad relationship and that was just the way it was. I was ready to call it a life.

One day a voice sounded off. NO. You can do this and you WILL do this. I listened to what God wanted me to do and God provided what I needed.

I got lots of work. I saved all the money I could save in a years' time and then bought myself the S-10. About the time I saved enough up to rent a place a friend told me about a house with a barn that may be for rent near where I grew up. It was and I had enough to rent it.

When it came time to move I didn't know how I would get the horses and goats to the new house. There was a knock at the door. It was a very good friend of mine who was Amish but showed up at the door in English cloths. He had left the Amish. He offered to find a trailer and haul the animals to the new farm for me.

So there we were, the kids and I in a new place.

The only furniture we had was one single sized bed, a mattress and our computers. No refrigerator. No microwave. No washer or dryer. No living room furniture. Nothing. I was the one to sleep on the floor because my bad decisions were not the kids fault. For a while we got a cooler and kept ice in it for milk and stuff and then we kept cold cuts in a camper fridge that someone let us borrow.

Despite the empty house, we were happy. For the first time in my life I had gone against what everyone thought I should do and did what my gut said and we were happy. Truly happy.

I worked hard and things started to fall into place. Someone had a refrigerator for sale that I could afford. We still have it to this day here at the farm. Someone else had a washer and dryer at a reasonable price. Someone was giving away a couch and a kitchen table. My parents were getting a new bed and offered their old one to me.

Within a year, I had the whole house set up to look like a home. For a year and a half the kids and I lived a life of peace and happiness. For me though, there was something missing. I knew it would take someone pretty strong, persistent and special to break through the wall I had up.

On August 16th 2008 I went to my parents' home to ride with them to a pig roast. They were often "my dates" when there were B-B-Q's or things to do. I was very man-sour and not needing or wanting anyone special in my life. I was content to go with them to gatherings.

My Mom used to try to convince me that everyone needs someone. "Not me." I'd say, in a very matter of fact tone while I shook my head no.

I'll never forget one such conversation. She said "Sometimes at night I'll feel your fathers hand on my back, just making sure I'm here." That melted my heart.

On that day as I be bopped into the house to see if they were ready to go, my Mother took me by the hand into their living room and lead me to "the wall of pictures."

There they were. Pictures of all my Brothers and Sisters with their Husbands and Wives. My picture was of my horse and me. I smiled.

"Lori, you need a person." She said.

Still to this day I don't know why I decided to drive separate from them and follow them to the pig roast. But I did.

Once there I ran into a friend or two. One was my friend Louie, setting up his band to play that night. The other was an old friend I used to work with at a gas station. I hadn't seen her in a few years. It was nice to see them and catch up. Feeling settled in and social, I decided to stay beyond the time my folks left for home.

Someone playing horse shoes across the lawn caught my eye. Big guy. Handsome guy. There was just something about him. I kept sneaking glances at him. At one point when I looked at him he was looking in my direction. Was he looking at me? I turned around. No one there.

He MUST have been looking at me.

I got involved in talking with a group of people and when I turned back to where he was playing shoes, he was gone. My eyes scanned the yard and all of people talking and laughing. He was nowhere in sight. He must have gone home. My heart sank. Too shy to just walk up and say hi, I had missed my chance.

"Darla, I'm going to head home now." I said to my friend. "NO! Stay, come dance with us!" "Okay, just for one song then I'm out of here." I said.

The song was a fast song and we all danced on the grass floor of the tent that night. Laughing. Letting off steam. Taking a break from life. Doing what you do when you dance.

I saw him coming out of the corner of my eye. My heart dropped. He had a girl with him and they were heading onto the green dance floor. He had a girlfriend? What a snake!" He made a point to walk close to me as they walked past. He turned to me and said "hi." Oh, even worse. How dare he flirt with me with his girlfriend right there!

Now I knew it was time to leave. I just wanted to go home. The song was ending and my friends and I were exiting the grass. The band started to play a slow song as I was saying my goodbyes to them.

I felt a hand on my arm. "Hey, do you want to dance?" It was him. Maybe that wasn't his girlfriend. I was confused and intrigued at the same time. I would find out. "Sure, I said."

As we danced a million questions were asked between us. His friends told him they thought that I was with the band guy they had seen me talking to earlier. I told him that I thought he was with the girl he was dancing with. Turned out she was the wife of a good friend.

We laughed at our previous game of cat and mouse and were interrupted by a loud voice that was familiar to both of us. "He's an ass hole Lori." It was my older Brother Steve dancing with his wife a short distance away.

We both learned that night what a small world it can be. Dan was a boss at the same company all three of my Brothers had, at one time in their lives, worked for. Two were still working there and knew Dan well.

The rest of the evening was spent dancing. Talking by the fire. Laughing.

At the stroke of midnight, just like Cinderella I said I had to go and I quickly made my way to my S-10. My daughter was alone at home and I promised not to leave her alone beyond a certain time.

Dan followed me to my truck and asked if he could see me again. I jotted my number down on a tiny piece of paper and went on my way. He called the next day and showed up at my house that very next night.

Sitting on the front porch on that warm August night drinking beers we learned more and more about each other's lives. He was going through a divorce and having a hard time with it. He was a "for better or worse" kind of man who had no choice in the matter. Being through it myself I related and felt much empathy. I switched to coffee while he kept drinking and talking his worries away. I intently listened to him and let him get it all out. When there was a break in his thought process he looked at me and nodded to the outside wall of the house.

"Wanna go in there and mess around?" What he said threw me. I laughed a loud laugh and said an even louder "No." He replied with "Wanna stay out here and mess around?" I shook my head from side to side. "No."

He sighed deep and lifted his arm to look at his watch. "Well, I have to work tomorrow, I guess I better get going."

He was a lost soul. I knew he was hurting and just as importantly, I knew he needn't be on the roads driving. I made him take a walk with me in the dark to sober up and by the end of the night he was asleep on the box of his truck, covered by a cab, parked down behind the barn.

As I lay in my own bed contemplating the night, I thought he would never call or come back again. I thought about everything he was about to go through when it came to his divorce. I told myself if he called again I wouldn't pick up the phone. But I did.

I sure enough gave him a run for his money. My attempts to deflect him didn't work. He was persistent and for some reason as much as I didn't want a relationship, I couldn't help but want to be with him. When he told me that he loved me I told him I was sorry. I couldn't say it back. Within time I knew that wall was crumbling.

When I was finally able to say it, it was a big emotional deal to me. Those are strong words.

His reply was "I know you do, you have loved me from the start."

On December 17th, 2010 we took my folks dinner. My famous lasagna. While we were eating Dan got down on one knee and asked me to marry him. Both of my parents smiles where as bright as smiles come. They both loved him. Yet they knew how independent I was. They were happy that I was able to let someone in.

I told my Mother, pick a date and I'll make it happen. "Valentine's Day." She said. Valentine's Day 2011 was on a Tuesday. I knew it might be difficult but a promise was a promise. I knew she picked a day close because although my Father hadn't been diagnosed yet, his health was failing.

The announcement I made to them in January brought head shaking smiles and a little laughter. A definite sense of no surprise at all, filled the air.

"Mom. Dad. We're getting married in the horse barn by the Mayor of Ulysses on Valentine's Day and Tyke is going to be the ring bearer."

We did just that. The mayor was a wonderful person with no problem at all in coming to the barn to marry us. A horse lover herself, she was excited at the idea. Her husband came with her. All of our kids and horses were there and we taped it for my folks to see.

It was unique. Special. Unforgettable.

At the time we had no clue that someday we would be living in Ulysses and I would see the Mayor often. She'd never forget that wedding in that barn that chilly February night. When she talked of it she always smiled. Me too.

Life's funny that way. Sometimes when you plan or even just wonder about where you'll be a few years down the road, you're all wrong. The road never stops winding. It never will.

My Mother passed away exactly four years to the month, day and even right down to the hour that Dan and I first met.

I found my person, Mom. That man who will put his hand on my back in the middle of the night just to make sure I'm still there.

Dan

18
The Letter

Things were about to change in the neighborhood. The bishop was moving to Ohio. One set of our Amish friends would be buying and moving into the Bishops farm. Another set of our Amish friends who were renting the farm above us, from the bishop, would be swapping homes with "the bad seed" who was buying that property. They would live there until fall, when the farm over the hill would be available for them to buy. We had so hoped they wouldn't move far. That young couple was a breath of fresh air to us. Kind and personable. Outgoing and friendly. Young and in love. We would enjoy their presence as our neighbors for as long as they were on this side of the hill. Even after that, we were sure they wouldn't become strangers.

There was one mover who was impatient. The bad seed. We could see he wasn't waiting.

Nice weather after a long cold winter had arrived. Dan and I started to enjoy walks with the animals. The two alpine boys we had, adored us and would follow us to the ends of the earth. That night they would walk with us. Up the road. Into the pasture to cross acres and acres of land leading back to the road. Homeward bound.

A big wagon was coming with two dogs trailing behind. "Is it him? Is it the bishop?" I said as our pace slowed. Dan focused on the wagon. The dogs were the bishop's dogs. The driver was the bad seed, moving a load of items to his new farm. We were uncertain of how the goats would react to the wagon and dogs. They stayed close to us as the bad seed approached. Once beside us, the wagon came to a slow stop. We did not. "Hi, how are you tonight?" He said.

Still walking I turned to look behind me for the goats. "Come on goats." I said. Without looking at him. Dan mumbled "alright." We kept walking. With a slight tap of the reins, he was on his way continuing up the hill.

Another of his son-in-laws, he was the bishops puppet in the farm purchase disaster. He was like a flea that you couldn't flick off. He came and took, took, took and walked away smiling about it with a cocky condescending grin. He tried to pick fights with Dan and poured stress on us like it was his job. No, we couldn't be the friendly neighbors we are to everyone else. He didn't deserve our friendship. His cocky smile would forever be etched in our heads.

Mail from the state investigation came sooner than thought. We weren't expecting it until early summer. I tore open the envelope and began to read.

"Following review this office has determined the circumstances in the case do not permit formal prosecution. Consequently, the file in this matter is closed."

The letter only mentioned the gas lease and didn't refer to any of the other complaints filed. What about their part in the black mail? What about the dishonesty? What about the sudden absence of phone calls and emails at the most crucial times during the sale? The legal advice to lock things up? What about that?

Stunned, I didn't understand. I needed to lay down and let the chanting begin. "Let go and let God." Over and over. I fell asleep for a very short while and thought about things, trying to figure out how they could have so much evidence and still find nothing wrong.

Simple. The real estate company was deceptive during the sale. They could bond together and all say the same thing. Who were Dan and I, really? We were nobodies in this game. We were nobodies then and we felt like we still were. Sure we had specific times and dates of conversations that took place but it wouldn't matter if they said those conversations never happened.

Aside from the OGM rights we guess the rest of what they put us through didn't matter either.

We were not allowed to see any details of the investigation or why they decided what they decided.

The only part of the letter that made me feel better was this.

"The very act of investigating a licensee can serve as a strong deterrent to professional misconduct. The information you provided will be kept on file and reference to it has been entered into an informal database so that it can be used by this office in the future to determine if there is a pattern of problems with this licensee."

The day went on with thoughts of "I just don't understand" roaming through my head.

I calmed down my mind and let my heart talk. We always do say "Everything for a reason." Maybe there was a reason for this.

If we had got the report we really expected to get, we would have taken them to court along with the Amish seller. Maybe we weren't meant to go through that. Maybe we had been saved from the expense and the time it would take. Maybe this was some sort of answer to us that we should put this part of it to rest now. We had done all we could do. It was the end of the road and time to let God be the judge and jury as far as the real estate went.

Let go and let God take care of it.

The following Monday I would call Galton PA and get small claims papers. We would file a claim against the seller and do things ourselves this time. When court was over, it would all be over.

One thousand dollars for cleaning the barn and the saw mill? That is what the seller reluctantly agreed to. Was he kidding?

Dan and I had spent the past entire year cleaning up the mess left behind. Dust masks and shovels and pitch forks and trips to the land fill. Diesel for the tractor and truck. We had at least one more summer to go before it would all be done. One thousand dollars would not be sufficient at all. It wasn't even a drop in the bucket.

It was April now and Dan was still driving the truck I bought while he worked on getting his own truck running. The bills for the parts were expensive and he just couldn't seem to get it in drivable condition.

We knew couldn't afford a lawyer so I would put on yet another hat. I would be our lawyer. I would plan our strategy. I would do the best I could.

I would print dozens of photographs and categorized them with each claim. I would scan through emails from the real estate and pin them to each corresponding claim. I would prove not giving us an extension was an intentional act. I would question an as-is sale to a contract sale.

If it was deemed an as-is sale, everything that was there when we agreed on a price should have stayed there and no further mess should have been made.

If the contract was deemed to be valid because of intentionally not giving us a second extension, everything should have stayed and the mess should have been cleaned up.

There was one thing that Dan and I were sure of. No matter what happened we would come out ahead.

The seller, if he chose to defend, would have to travel that four hundred and fifty miles and probably would have to pay a lawyer to help him.

We, on the other hand, only had a twenty mile trip to court. We had done absolutely nothing wrong and had no concerns on a counter suite.

The small claims forms would be in the mail soon and we would fill them out and send them back. In no time at all we would have a court date.

We never responded to the sellers last letter. Our thoughts were that he probably thought we gave up. We did not. We were sure he would be quite surprised at the next registered letter containing court papers he would receive.

This one would mean definite business. No more chances to make things right.

The form arrived with filing instructions. We couldn't go over the jurisdictional limit without it going to a higher court. A higher court would mean we should have a lawyer. A lawyer would mean time and money we did not have. We felt our only choice was to cut down what we were asking for, to stay within the limit. In PA the limit is $12,000.

I sat down and began to write a summation for the court form. So much had happened that it was hard to keep brief. For three nights I went back to it to reread and revise. We only had one shot at this. I couldn't spout off in a frantic unorganized way. I knew I had to keep to the basics and keep such a complicated case as simple as I could.

Finally, I was satisfied.

"In June 2012 we agreed on a sale price with the farms owners, for their farm. Three of the selling points to us were the fenced in yard, the metal fence in the pasture and the shelving in the Amish store.

Due to FHA regulations we had to put electric in the house to obtain the loan. The sellers agreed and gave us an extension. After the electric was in, the bank told us we had to put in heat and plumbing to get the loan. It took four months to close.

Between the times we agreed on a price, and closing, approx. 50 sheep roamed the barn/fields breaking boards in the barn.

The saw mill was trashed with rubbish thrown everywhere, the fencing in front of the house was ripped up and taken.

We complained and although the sale went through, we feel the seller intentionally did not give us a second extension because he felt it would prevent him from being held accountable for the horrific mess he left behind for us to clean up.

Right before closing we were made to write a statement to the sellers saying that we did not want the Amish store shelving or the metal fence panels, or the deal would be off.

We had almost $15,000 in utilities into the house. We could not lose it. We had no choice but to write the statement.

We were left with a mortgage that included paying for the things that were taken.

We were left with two to three feet of manure and other trash that covered 3/4 of the barn floor. A rat infested grain bin full of moldy grain. A hay mow with a room full of 8" thick rotted chicken poop and broken doors, windows, mattresses and old rusty useless equipment. The sewer was left full. A 2' pile of soot was left behind in the basement from their wood stove. The saw mill was trashed with garbage. The land was scattered with glass, nails, broken plastic, pipes, boards, animal bones, etc."

We were asking for:

Lawyer fees for a settlement offer made in 2013.
Full sewer we paid to get pumped.
Barn, sawmill, house and land debris clean up.
December 2012 to October 2013, a low average of 360 hours over the span of 11 months.
(Non-burnable) Land fill costs.
Diesel used for truck and tractor during clean up.
Metal fencing taken. **(Depreciated value)**

Fencing/gate that fenced house in. **(Depreciated value)**
12 Metal Shelving units approx. 38" x 18" x 84" each unit. **(Depreciated value)**

$11,979.20

Once I was confident in my organization I had Dan sign the papers along beside my name. The next day I would drive to the municipal court to file the claim and get the ball rolling on our attempt to get justice.

To my surprise I was able to stand there and wait while the documents were filed and a court date was set.

May 7, 2014. 2:30 in the afternoon.

The bishops son-in-law and the bishops daughter would both receive a registered letter with the complaint and court date within a week.
Those letters would arrive to them the same week as the Bishops auction. Chances where, they would be attending the auction.

In my heart I felt sympathy for the bishops Daughter. In the one time I met her she seemed oblivious to the dirty deeds done by her father and Husband. I had to remind myself this wasn't a woman to woman thing. She seemed to have a preserved innocence and loyal thoughts about things and she probably always would have.

We wondered what their reaction would be. Did they think that if they ignored the whole thing we would go away? If they did, they were wrong.

In our thoughts we wondered, what is Karma, anyway? How does it happen? Would it come quicker for bishops son in law and daughter than it did for him?

There were so many people with bad experiences from dealing with the bishop. He had driven away other Amish families. He had angered the local English with his crooked ways.

Now that he was moving, were they thinking that karma finally paid him a visit? That what went around finally came around for him?

Because of him, we became stronger. Strong enough to stand up to him and strong enough to expose him. To end his power trip. For us and for those before us he had wronged.

19
Puppy Rumspringa

The view from the left window of my art room changed. Wagon loads of farm equipment started to arrive early in the week and settle into the land across the road from our home. Rows of rakes. Wagons. Cement blocks. Odds and ends. A hay elevator. Wooden sheep ramps and hay bines. A grain bin and even a row boat with large buggy wheels attached to it.

By weeks end the field was full with several items lined up and waiting to be auctioned off that Saturday. A tent was put up. Tables and folding chairs were set out for popcorn and baked goods sales.

Traffic had picked up profusely and early birds stopped beside the road to look over the treasures being auctioned the next day.

Dan and I had been at the barn tending to

Pepper who was injured from a kick. After settling him in and making sure he was comfortable we walked to the house, smiling and waving at a passerby who beeped. As I looked up I saw several rows of fencing across the road on the horizon. I elbowed Dan. "Hey, there's our fence." He returned my glance and replied "I hope he thinks it was worth it."

Once inside I started making us dinner and we both started discussing what was about to happen. The auction and the bishop moving away. This was a big deal.

"You know, people are going to be wondering why the leader of a community is moving. They will be asking him and others why he is leaving. They are all going to point at this farm and us."

"I know." I said. "But it wasn't us. We are not why he is leaving. HE is why he's leaving. In the past year we have heard so many people say what a crooked person he is. Not just English people. Amish people too. There is such anger in the voices of some of the English people. We know why. He was so condescending and cocky to us. He was on a power trip and now he has been knocked off his high horse. Maybe we were his karma. Maybe this is some sort of vindication for all the others he has taken advantage of. We

184

stood our ground. We exposed him. The reason he is moving isn't because of us. It's because he thought he was invincible and could continue on the path he was walking. History didn't repeat itself this time. We didn't lick our wounds and move on. We called him out on his actions and he took a fall that has been a long time coming."

Dan looked at me and smiled that supportive smile. "You're right."

The day was bright and sunny. Not a typical day for early April in Northern PA. Perfect day for an auction. Cars and trucks with trailers lined the dirt road in both directions. The hill came alive with people walking past the farm. It seemed many of the auction goers were Amish traveling in English driven vehicles.

Straw hats milled around the equipment and when the auctioneer started to speak they grouped together in a tight circle and moved from item to item. A swarm of straw hats. An occasional yell with a bid. I could hear it all. I could see it all, from my open art room window.

How could I not help but feel responsible for what was going on across the road? I assured myself I did the right thing. When faced with a bad man I did not cower. I did not retaliate with violence. I did not seek vengeance in a physical way. I never raised my voice. I did what my gut told me to do and I did it to help others. Would it help others? He was moving away to another state. Would he do the same sort of things to his new neighbors and to people he came to know there as he did to people here or would he think twice about his actions? He might never have cared how his actions affect others but this time his actions bit him in the butt.

Would he be concerned about that in the future? Would he continue on this journey of hurting others for his own benefit or would he have learned an important lesson?

I would never forget how he treated me like I was beneath him. I would never forget that cocky smile and the look in his eyes when he glanced at me like I was no better than the lowest form of life on earth. I would never forget the lack of compassion from him and how he took advantage of our absence while we were at my Mothers viewing and funeral. I would never forget the desperation. The angst and the turmoil Dan and I felt at his hands when he had us under his thumb. When he controlled our future and there wasn't a thing we could do about it.

Now, he would never forget us.

Dan came home after work and with a smile and a hug he grabbed a beer. I joined him with a cup of coffee. We sat there for hours watching the event. Listening to the auctioneer over the speaker, being carried by an Amish man. His loud rambling voice ringing clearly to us from the land across the road as he put a price on each item in the rows of machinery and what not's. We talked to passersby who stopped to chat. We reflected on the past.

Late that afternoon our children joined us. We all talked and laughed and played with the dogs and goats on the side porch. It was a subtle celebration of an unexpected page being turned.

The crowd across the road thinned and auction items were being hauled away. Cars and trucks with trailers were leaving a little at a time. One of them stopped to talk to Dan explaining he came to haul for anyone who needed something hauled. He had no takers. He had seen a dryer and freezer out behind our house from the road and asked if we would like them hauled away. Yes!

Our dryer stopped working over the winter and we had to get a new one. The freezer was big and old and had been defrosted and set outside to clear room for the work Dan had started in the cellar. They were eye sores and we had no idea what we would do with them. It would cost money to take them to the dump and time and money to take them somewhere to scrap. We would deal with when we had time. We were happy to give them away for scrap. We were thankful that the right person at the right time came along.

The next day was more beautiful than the last. Dan and I spent most of it outside enjoying the warm sunshine. I gathered up pieces of boards and sticks Roxy had carried into the yard and abandoned. I overturned water troths and buckets at the barn that had been frozen into hot beds made by the goats. I was wiping away the remnants' of winter a little at a time when I heard Dan yell to me.

"Lori, call Roxy! Keep her at the barn, there's a dog coming down the road!"

Roxy had become rather a pest when it came to traffic on foot or if a strange dog came along. Off to the road she would go and her listening ears went mute every time. She would attach herself to walkers and tag along hopping beside them with a wiggle and a wag. If another dog came along she felt it was her job to chase them off away from "her" farm.

I stood calling to her to come to the barn while Dan yelled at her trying to chase her away from himself and toward me. She sat between us not knowing what to do. The solution was for him to grab her collar and put her in the mow of the barn, closing the door behind him to save any standoff there may be. From the panic of Dan's actions I expected a large dog to run toward us from the road, on a mission to fight. One that Roxy may have trouble running off without getting herself hurt.

When the commotion slowed a tiny being walked onto the farm. She looked like a tiny jack Russell mix. She was dusty yellow in color with big brown eyes that could win your heart in an instant. Dan's heart melted as he picked her up. He let Roxy out of the mow to teach her to be nice to animals that were smaller than herself.

The pup held her own as we watched her sweet angelic face turn to an evil snarl whenever Roxy got to close.

The little dog pranced around the farm all day. As I was giving my car a wash she made herself at home by jumping in to curl up on the passenger seat until I was done. When she wasn't with me she was in the garage with Dan as he continued to work on his truck.

We assumed she was an Amish dog and would find her way home but by night fall she was still on the farm with us, sitting on our side porch watching the buggies come home from church that evening.

I was sure she would run after one of them but she never moved a muscle as she watched them go by. When we went in for the night, we left her outside with an occasional walk to the door to see if she was still there. She was. Curled up tightly in a little ball on that porch. We wondered if she planned to be there all night. We couldn't stand the thought of her getting hit if she wandered off looking for her home in the dark, so after a while we brought her into the house with us.

"We might have to keep her" Dan said has he cradled her. I could see he had fallen in love.

I replied "She has a collar. Looks to be Amish made. I'll bet she has a home. I'll take her tomorrow and go looking for where she belongs. For now, she needs a bath."

I drew a warm bath and removed the wide leather collar from her neck. She seemed to enjoy the thick lather from the baby shampoo I was using and stayed still has I massaged the soap into her thick beige fur.

Once I had rinsed and dried her off, I swaddled her in a towel and asked Dan to take her while I cleaned up the bathroom. She was shivering as I watched Dan hold her tightly against his chest assuring her she would be okay.

I got a fresh towel and took the pup from Dan's arms and to my art room with me and then settled her on the floor in a towel nest, while Dan laid on the couch to watch TV. She didn't stay with me. Off to the couch she went and with one quick leap she was cuddled as close into Dan as she could get, burying her head between his neck and shoulder.

"Honey, can you get a blanket for her?" He said. "Sure." I took a blanket to him to cover his new friend and within minutes they were both fast asleep in front of the TV.

When it came time for Dan to migrate upstairs to go to bed for the night, he brought her to me and she laid quietly at my feet and sat in my lap while I worked, only getting into mischief once when she stole my lip balm and tried to eat the packaging.

When it came time for me to go to bed I wasn't sure what to do with her. I took her with me.

That night the little pup laid between both our heads on a pillow.

Dreaming sweet dreams, she never woke once.

I was obligated to find the little lost dog's owner and I did just that the next morning. It was a Monday. I put her in my car and knocked on a door or two in the neighborhood as she happily rode along in the passenger seat. It wasn't long before I knew where she belonged.

I pulled onto her owners' driveway and saw a young girl with a hoe working a short distance away in a flower bed. With the pup under one arm I got out of the car and walked toward her.

"Is this yours?" I said while petting the dog now cuddled deep into both my arms. The young lady stopped working and smiled. "Yes, she is ours. She followed Dads wagon to the auction Saturday and didn't come back home with him. We have been trying to get her not to follow behind us when we leave but now and then she does anyway"

I smiled and set the dog down gently on the ground. "She's such a good little dog. My Husband really likes her." I said.

The dog pranced away down the sidewalk, like

she had never missed a beat. Zig zagging between bushes and plants, stopping for a whiff of this and a whiff of that.

I said my goodbyes and she thanked me.

As I drove away I had to chuckle. That little Amish pup got the works. A day of playing and pets, a full belly, a spa treatment, a night of watching TV on the couch and then bedtime brought her two warm bodies to cuddle with all night long.

It was a puppy Rumspringa.

Auction Goers

20

It Was Karma

Spring was coming in slow fashion and the warm days were far and few. With no run in shelter yet, and no leaves on the trees for the animals to take cover from the cold rain, I found myself more and more waking up in the wee hours and laying there listening to what I knew was an icy cold rain storm, until I couldn't take knowing the animals were out there in it. I would get out of bed, get dressed and taking a battery operated lantern my cousin got us for a house warming gift, I'd head to the pasture in the rain to put the animals inside.

I always came back wet and shivering but it was only then, when I knew they were tucked in safe and dry, that I could fall asleep in peace.

There had to be a better way. On the first nice day I would go to the sugar shack and clear the boards from the porch attached to it, so the animals would have cover.

I did just that. Roxy, the two alpine goats and I walked down to the shack on a bright, sunny and doable weather wise day. I put on my pink work gloves and tossed board after board to one end of the porch, careful to look for nails. When I finished I looked around in disgust. Although we had cleaned the pasture the previous spring, it seemed more and more junk was appearing. I pulled up three garden hoses from the ground. Broken buckets. Pieces of glass.

As I was collecting junk I saw Bo, our mischievous Alpine, from the corner of my eye. He was pulling up some sort of plastic that had been buried tightly beside the shack.

"Bo, what do you have now?" I said as I moved toward him. With my work gloves still on I reached for the plastic and started to pull it out of the weeds and dirt. A white garbage bag. With another tug it ripped and some of the contents fell out.

I crouched down to run my gloved hands through the lost treasures among shards of broken glass. A child's green necklace and bracelet set. A pink teething ring. A yellow duck attached to a bracelet. Several pink plastic safety pins. The same sort of trinkets I had seen in the trinket jar I used as a reference earlier that year. I didn't understand. Why were they thrown out and why there, down in the pasture by the sugar shack?

I picked up the broken glass, paper plates, chip bags and other garbage and headed home with an extra bag I had brought to collect bones, as I made my way back to the house.

As I picked up skull after skull, leg bones, joints, parts and pieces of every farm animal imaginable I thought to myself, this is never going to end, is it? How many years will we have to go before stuff stops coming up from the land?

As I was nearing the house I saw two semis pull into the bishop's driveway. They backed their trailers in and left them there. A moving company. The time had arrived.

The next day buggy's came and went from his farm. We assumed they were helping him to pack up.

Dan and I were outside by the garage when those semis came back to pick up the trailers. We stood there in silence watching as they pulled out of the drive and turned onto the road, Ohio bound.

We wondered if the seller would try to settle for a higher amount than $1,000 before the court date, show up for court or ignore the court date all together.

I scanned the web for anything to do with the Amish and law suits. Everything I read said they do not participate in or believe in our court system.

Most searches said the Amish strongly believe in the message Jesus Christ delivered in the Sermon on the Mount:

"Resist not evil, but whoever shall smite thee on thy right cheek, turn to him the other also" (Matthew 5:39).

I had to keep in the back of my mind that this whole thing was all about bad Amish not living up to their reputations. No matter what I read about the Amish and their way of life, none of it matched up to the way the bishop and his son-in-law acted.

We got a letter from the court. The sellers would be there to defend. My only thought at the moment was, bring it on.

I wouldn't dig right in to the work of preparing for the case. I would think of our strategy while I as driving to town. While I was taking a long bath. While I was laying in bed ready to drift off to sleep.

Sometimes my mind would wander. What if he brings a lawyer? What if he brings the real estate people and the bishop and they all get together and lie, just like they did all through the sale?

Those thoughts never stayed. A calm voice inside me always quickly told me I would do just fine. I could counter every single dishonest sentence that came from their mouths, with physical proof.

As the time for court drew near I felt myself getting nervous. Time was a week away. Late nights working became stressful. Not because of court. Maybe I watch too many crime shows. People have been offed for much less than $12,000.

I kept my uneasiness to myself. Every window I passed in the wee hours of the morning gave me a weak feeling that I fought with reminding myself that I was in Gods hands and if anything ever did happen to me or to our farm there would be swarms of people pointing fingers in one direction. I didn't want my imagination to get the best of me but it had become a struggle for me to shake it. I carried that fear with me day after day and shook it off day after day.

Part of shaking it off in such a stressful situation where things felt so tense was a long haired black and white cat who had become accustom to late night attention when the house was still and quiet and dark. She'd come out from where she had decided to hide for that day. Out from under a bed. Out from the back of an upstairs closet. She'd wander into my art room where she knew her food and I would be.

I used to tell my Mother I loved how she smelled when I hugged her hello or goodbye. She didn't wear perfume so her and I had decided it was the fabric softener she used. Now and then that same strong scent would become abundantly clear with a leap onto my lap from Princess in the early morning hours when she came to me to collect her dinner, her hugs and her whisker rubs. Whenever that happened my world always seemed to feel like everything would be alright, no matter what.

Court was less than a week away. Time had gone by so quickly and my thoughts were endlessly turning with still no voice inside me that said I was ready to get the physical evidence together. I was told to think. Think. Think.

Think some more.

Even with confidence and positive thoughts pulsing through my veins I had to remind myself more than a few times that things don't always go the way we think they should go. Sometimes it doesn't matter how much time and effort you put into something. If things don't turn out as you had planned there is a reason for it.

A day before court it was time. Time to put all those thoughts about how to proceed, to paper. I put down my paintbrushes and picked up a pen and piece of paper about 10 PM that night.

Before I knew it the sun was coming up. Dan woke up to a kitchen table full of time stamped photographs. Contracts. Receipts. Emails. Those hand written letters from the seller. A time line with dates to guide me through our story as I would tell it to the Judge. Exhausted as I was, there would be no sleep until I felt secure that I was no less than absolutely ready to prove what happened to us was intentional and wrong.

I laid down on the couch that morning about 6:00 AM and Dan woke me at 11:00 AM.

Just enough time to look over everything again for my own peace of mind before taking a quick shower.

I had sold a couple books from my friend Kathie's boutique. Not having many nice cloths to chose from, I used the money from one of the books to buy a new shirt to wear to court. It would go well with the black jeans Dan had bought me the previous Christmas.

I gathered up all of the evidence from the kitchen table and organized them into folders. It was time to go.

The ride to Galton PA always felt so long. This time the trip felt short. My mind was preoccupied. Who would be there? Would the bishop be there? The realty? Would he have a lawyer to try to trip me up? Would he even show up? That still voice inside told me to be calm. I could do this. No matter what. I had everything I needed.

As we pulled into the drive way we saw a car with Ohio plates. At least one of our questions was answered. They were there. But whos cars where the others?

We went inside to the small quaint court and at a quick glance saw a few people in a waiting area. Not turning around to get full view, I wondered who they were.

The Judge came and summoned us to sit in her court room. The seller and his wife sat in the defendant seats. Gone was that sharply dressed couple who came to our door the previous June. Her with her wholesome looks and he with his cocky attitude and condescending demeanor. Now there they sat quietly in every day Amish attire. Not dressed for court as they would dress for church or a social gathering.

Two English sat behind them, further back in the courts folding chairs. I assumed one was their driver, but who was the other? He wasn't a lawyer. They sat there alone.

I was out of my element. I had never done anything like this before and I was nervous as I approached the stand to be sworn in. "I swear to tell the truth, the whole truth and nothing but the truth, so help me God." As I sat down and began to pull the time line from my files I felt my hands shaking and prayed to collect myself as I gave the Judge times and dates of occurrences. My mind wasn't staying with me, it was jumping ahead at times and my preoccupation seemed to be taking over. And then, I thought of my daughter sitting behind Dan in one of those fold up chairs in the back of the room.

I had to show her how strong a woman can be. I had to show her how to have confidence and poise in the most stressful of situations.

I thought of my Mother, who passed that poise on to me. I thought of my father, who always fought for what was right.

I regained composure and was led to explaining our case piece by piece. Photograph by photograph. Email by email. I was on that stand for well over an hour telling our story with an occasional trip to the defendants table at the request of the judge so that they could see our evidence after she had seen it.

It was the sellers turn to approach the stand. "I swear to tell the truth, the whole truth and nothing but the truth..." There was silence as I watched the tall young Amish man sightly sway and shrug. "That's alright" The Judge said.

Just as I shook with nerves, he did too. His shakiness never stopped. His story had holes and back tracks and a lot of it just plain didn't make sense. He claimed the value of the 13 heavy duty metal shelves taken from the store was only $100. He claimed he value of the 350 feet of sheep fence ripped from the ground was only

$100. We had printed estimates for replacements that proved otherwise.

He wasn't on the stand for very long and before we knew it, it was time for closing statements. The judge asked him "What do you think you owe them" In response he said "We'd be willing to pay them $1,000 but it took us $600 to travel here from Ohio. I guess we could give them $500."

It was all we could do to contain our thoughts from coming out of our mouths. Was he kidding? We should be responsible for his trip to come to court?

The judge turned to us. Why do you think I should rule in your favor?

I spoke up. "Because we are paying a mortgage on things we don't own and because we don't feel we should be responsible for cleaning up a mess that we didn't make."

The judge explained she had three days to make her decision and we would receive the judgement by mail. Court was over. We'd know the answer in few days. I took a deep breath. Court was adjourned.

As we walked to the car Dan turned to me "I'm

proud of you, you did so good!!"

Now it was a waiting game. I would be waiting on the couch. The stress and the anticipation and the all nighter the night before knocked me off my feet. Sick. Real sick. I would stay on the couch until almost two days later until I finally felt good enough to get up and move around. Laying there I wondered, could I have done anything different. Anything better?

I thought of pictures I had forgotten to take to court with us. There were questions I should have asked him, I didn't ask, that he would have struggled to answer truthfully. I had to keep reminding myself it was no longer in my hands and that I had done okay.

Court was on a Wednesday. It was Friday evening. We weren't expecting to get any mail for a few days.

I was able that day to get started back to work on my art orders and the night had flown by so quickly. Normally in the wee hours when the paintbrush had been put down for the night I'd surf the web to wind down before going upstairs. Maybe to find the answer to a question. Maybe to look up a term. Maybe to get song lyrics.

I had remembered that I found the court date

for us online shortly after I filed, in the county public records. Would I be able to find the judgement if it had been decided? Did I want to? There had been so many disappointments in the past couple years and what felt like such unfairness, was I really ready for another slam if the judgement wasn't what we expected?

Yes, I was ready. With those disappointments came grace and strength. Good or bad, if the judgement was to be found, I needed to face it and put an end to the "I could have said this or should I have said that" in court.

I pulled up the county court site and slid a piece of paper out from a pile of papers on my desk. The piece of paper with the docket number on it.

I typed the number in and pushed the enter key. There it was. Open as file.

As I scanned the docket the first words I saw were "case closed." The second words "Judgement for the Plaintiff." The judgement was for the full amount. All I could do was stare. It wasn't sinking in.

My heart skipped a beat and a rush of adrenaline came over me as I intently scanned the computer screen once more. I felt the pressure of tears building up from behind my eyes as a lump formed in my throat. I heard myself say "It's over. Thank you so much God, oh thank you Lord Jesus."

The tears never did come as I popped up from my chair in the wee hours of that morning and ran up the stairs and own the hall to our bedroom where Dan was sleeping.

"DAN!! DAN!! WE WON!! WE WON!! THE FULL AMOUNT!" A quick waking Dan thinking something was wrong suddenly came to, realizing what I said. Really?! The full amount!? "YES!" I exclaimed.

I printed the judgement out and laid it on the table for him to see.

It was over.

Karma comes around for the good as well as the bad. It goes hand in hand with everything happening for a reason.

There was a reason I didn't ride with my parents to that pig roast on that Summer night in 2008.

There was a reason the only available person to marry Dan and I was a Mayor in a town we'd someday live in.

There was a reason God brought that Amish couple into our lives. We would become friends and over a year later, they would buy the Bishops farm.

There was a reason that little black and white cat showed up from nowhere when I needed her most, after disappearing for a year without a trace.

There was a reason Tyke passed away before that long, brutally cold, brutally hard winter.

There was a reason Dan wasn't driving my little S-10 truck when he hit that black ice.

There was a reason the neighborhood seemed new and wonderful and more alive than ever.

We weren't the reason. I wasn't the reason.

It was karma.

"All that is necessary for the triumph of evil is that good men do nothing."
~Edmund Burke

We have a lot of work left to do here on the farm.

Please join us on Face Book

Amish Above the Law

We'll be updating our progress as the months and years continue on.